I WRITE ABOUT
SPORTS

I WRITE ABOUT
SPORTS

A COLLECTION OF SPORTSWRITING FROM COBB COUNTY
AND AROUND THE STATE OF GEORGIA,
FROM THE PAGES OF THE MARIETTA DAILY JOURNAL

JOHN BEDNAROWSKI

Deeds Publishing | Athens

Published by Deeds Publishing in Athens, GA
www.deedspublishing.com

Printed in The United States of America

Cover design by Mark Babcock.

ISBN 978-1-950794-23-2

Books are available in quantity for promotional or premium use. For information, email info@deedspublishing.com.

First Edition, 2020

10 9 8 7 6 5 4 3 2 1

For Mo,
who allows me to watch sports for a living.

CONTENTS

FOREWORD

As a point of reference, I am not officially a member of the staff of the Marietta Daily Journal but I have been around the paper long enough that I consider myself a part of the family, albeit the weird cousin who shows up at the family reunion with gravy stains on his tie.

I am proud to have a small role in the MDJ's daily life, although I am sure there are days that management could do without the honor when the phone starts ringing about one of my unvarnished opinions. I suffer fools poorly and it occasionally shows.

But whether you agree with me or my opinions, fret over a headline or a particular story, know that a lot of hard work by a lot of hard-working people goes into putting out the paper each and every day. Journalism has been called "literature in a hurry" and that it is.

The MDJ does its daily literature in a hurry and does it well. Perhaps no better example can be found than in and on the sports pages. The paper is not inclined to toot its own horn, so I will toot it for them.

To wit: John Bednarowski, the MDJ's sports editor has just finished his term as president of the Associated Press Sports Editors, a 400-plus member organization composed of the leading lights in the sports world, such as the New York Times, the Washington Post, USA Today, ESPN and the Boston Globe, to name just a few. Bednarowski is only the second Georgian to have headed the prestigious 46-year-old association and represents the smallest newspaper to have had a president of APSE. That, folks, is high cotton.

The organization just wound up its annual summer convention, this year in Atlanta, and the Marietta Daily Journal was one of 10 papers in the nation to win the Triple Crown for Best Daily Sports Section, Best Sunday Section and Best Special Section. Other winners included such heavyweights as The New York Times, Los Angeles Times, the Boston Globe, the Washington Post and the Seattle Times. The high cotton just keeps getting higher.

Awards are nothing new for Bednarowski. He had his own personal Triple Crown this year, winning Best Column from the Associated Press Managing Editors, Best Sports Writing from the Georgia Sports Writers Association and Best Sports Column from the Georgia Press Association.

When not winning awards, Bednarowski has been keenly focused on the future of sports reporting, particularly diversity. APSE has a program called Diversity Fellows. Even though he is now a past-president of the organization, he is busy helping establish the APSE Foundation, which will help provide education and funding opportunities for these young people who aspire to be sports editors one day, allowing them to network with professionals throughout the year at meetings and workshops.

Getting access to coaches and players these days is becoming more of an issue with sports writers. During his term as president of the APSE, Bednarowski was involved in getting a basketball beat writer's access restored by Bradley University in Peoria, Illinois. The school had restricted his access because they felt the reporter didn't "promote the Bradley brand." It is Bednarowski's opinion—and mine—that it is not the role of a reporter to promote a brand. It is a reporter's job to report. (Bradley University relented and apologized.)

Bednarowski, a native of northern Ohio, came to the Marietta Daily Journal in 2006, after graduation from the University of Alabama at

Birmingham. He had at one time thought he would be a history teacher until he found a niche writing sports for the UAB school paper. That led to a job in Pell City, Alabama, as a sportswriter, and then the Gadsden Times.

"I heard about an opening in Marietta and decided to check it out," he recalls. "I told my wife, Mo, she could do some shopping in Atlanta while we were in town. When I got to the MDJ, I suggested she wait in the car while I ran in. Three-and-a-half hours later, I walked out with the job. I am lucky she didn't kill me." We are all lucky.

So, what is next? After five years as a national officer and a year as president of the Associated Press Sports Editors, Bednarowski is back at his desk putting together the MDJ's annual 200-page (give or take) football preview magazine, due out in August. There is not a better one in the country. How good is it? "The Los Angeles Times asked if I would share a copy with them," he smiles.

The Marietta Daily Journal rightfully refers to itself as "Cobb's Local News Source Since 1886." In addition, John Bednarowski has managed to put himself and the MDJ in the company of the nation's elite media sports organizations as well.

I may only be the weird cousin who shows up at the family reunion with gravy stains on my tie, but I couldn't be prouder of my newspaper family and the people who make it go.

—**Dick Yarbrough,**
MDJ's Bednarowski Sports a National Reputation
July 2, 2019

COLLEGE FOOTBALL

DOOLEY PREACHES LEADERSHIP OFF FIELD, APRIL 26, 2007

Truth be told, a pig held the key to Georgia's 1980 national championship team.

At least that was the story former Bulldogs' football coach and athletic director Vince Dooley said while addressing the Cobb Chamber of Commerce's South Cobb Area Council on Wednesday at the Coach George E. Ford Center in Powder Springs.

The 74-year-old Dooley was speaking about leadership and being in leadership situations when he brought up the subject of the now infamous pig "crisis."

Spring practice was winding down in 1980 and the players were planning a party—a tradition at Georgia signifying the end of the grueling spring sessions. This particular year a handful of key players—all seniors—decided to make this the best end of spring practice party ever. It was to be a pig roast, the problem was there was no money to purchase said pig—hence the crisis.

So, they stole one.

"The problem was, it was a university pig," Dooley said. "When I found out about it I was really mad. Even more, the person in charge of the university pig was real mad, too."

The perpetrators were cornerback Scott Woerner, rover Chris Welton, linebacker and captain Frank Ros, center Hugh Nall and offensive lineman Nat Hudson.

"Hudson was the only one fast enough and strong enough to catch the pig," Dooley joked.

The coach pleaded with the administrator in charge of the university agriculture department to allow him to handle the situation himself, pledging he would not be sorry.

"Sometimes in situations, there are times when you can say too much," he said. "I should have left it at that, but then I said, 'And besides, these are five of the best people on the team.'"

He said he could tell then he should have stopped because he could tell what the man was thinking, "If this is five of your best you are in trouble."

The lesson Dooley said he learned was not to make a quick emotional decision. By waiting a few days before directing punishment he was able to remove the emotion. For the players, they probably wished for the emotional one.

"I could have kicked them off the team. Instead what I did was took them off scholarship. Then I had them paint the fence around the field everyday during the summer from 1 p.m. to 4 p.m.," Dooley said, noting that the summer of 1980 had a record 22 consecutive days of 100-degree temperatures. "It took them nearly the whole summer and when they finished they came up to me to tell me they were done and I said, 'It looks like it could use a second coat.'"

Dooley added that Woerner, Welton, Ros, Nall and Hudson were the main players, but everyone on the team was guilty. The team paid restitution for the ill-gotten sow, both on and off the field. But to this day he agreed with the late Erk Russell—Dooley's long-time defense coordinator—believing it was this fiasco that helped bring the team together laying the foundation for the undefeated championship season. Also, the second chance the players earned was laying a foundation for successful careers after college.

Woerner is a teacher in Rabun County. Welton worked with former Bulldog star Billy Payne to help bring the Olympics to Atlanta. He went on to become president of Meridian Management the marketing representative of the International Olympic Committee and is now CEO of Helios Partners Inc.

Ros is the Assistant Vice President for Latin Affairs for Coca Cola. Nall is the offensive line coach at Auburn University and Hudson went on to play for the New Orleans Saints and the Tampa Bay Buccaneers.

Other nuggets from the former coach:

- Dooley said things had changed considerably over his 40 years at the University of Georgia. He mentioned the increase in athletic budget from $2.5 million in 1964 to over $70 million today and the increase in Sanford Stadium from 43,000 to over 92,000, but the biggest change?

"When I started at the University my total package paid me $15,000 a year, now we have coaches making over $2 million."

- Looking back on last year's Bulldogs, he said the 9-4 off year could be pinned on an inexperienced quarterback, Matthew Stafford, getting thrown into a situation where he was in over his head. But he added the last three games, when Georgia beat ranked opponents, showed how far Stafford had come and how good he could be in the future.
- That said, Dooley is not sure what to expect out of the 2007 squad.

"Last year we had an experienced offensive line and a young quarterback. This year we have an experienced quarterback and an inexperienced offensive line."

Which would he prefer? "I'd rather have the experienced line," he said.

- On the University of Alabama having over 92,000 for its spring game, he said, "It reflects hope (in the program). They are probably tired after being beaten five years in a row by Auburn."
- About the success of Georgia's rival Florida is having right now with national championships in football and basketball, he said, "We were fortunate when I coached to have good success against Florida," Dooley said. "Their payback was overdue, but now they are taking it to an extreme."

COMMITTEE ONLY A FORMALITY AS KSU FOOTBALL AWAITS, DECEMBER 13, 2009

It came at the end of Kennesaw State's news conference Thursday announcing Vince Dooley, the former University of Georgia coach and athletic director would chair a 33-member exploratory committee to gauge the interest of bringing football to the Cobb County campus.

While people were shaking hands and talking about the possibilities of Owls football, a picture of the potential program's helmet appeared on a video screen behind the stage.

Underneath the black and gold helmet, it said, "Still undefeated."

The image was meant as a humorous way to wrap up the proceedings, but what it represented was just one of many signs that football at KSU is a done deal.

First, follow the money. University president Daniel Papp said he hopes football can happen, but "it depends on the finances."

Well, Kennesaw State has completed $400 million of real estate projects over the last four years. And, the university is currently in the second year of a five-year, $75 million fundraising project specifically for athletics. That project, despite the country being in the worst recession in decades, has already passed the $50 million mark.

Any football fundraising will be separate and above the current project, but if recent history is any indication, KSU should not have any problems getting support to make the Owls' program a reality.

Especially since Papp said that any place he goes to speak, the first question asked is always, "So, when is KSU going to get football?"

Second, and maybe more importantly, nothing outside a bad crop of tomatoes in his prized garden is going to fail under Dooley's watch. He is not going to lend his name or his efforts for almost a year to something that is not going to come to fruition. Any doubt was eliminated Thursday as soon as Dooley was photographed wearing a Kennesaw State hat and he said, "I'm proud to be an Owl."

So, if the 77-year-old Dooley—the most beloved Bulldog of them all who led Georgia to a national championship and built its athletic department into what it is today—is willing to make football a reality at Kennesaw State, what kind of football will it be?

A big hint came a week earlier when Kennesaw State announced its partnership with the new Women's Professional Soccer team, the Atlanta Beat. The university unveiled plans for a $16.5 million, 8,300-seat soccer stadium—and then added that it could expand to as much as 22,000 to accommodate football.

A stadium that seats anywhere from 10,000-22,000 guarantees KSU will not be a BCS school, and it likely will not be a member of the Football Bowl Subdivision in a non-BCS conference either. It also means the program will likely be bigger than an NAIA Shorter or a Division III LaGrange.

In the end, it leaves KSU playing either Division II football or joining the Football Championship Subdivision, formerly known as Division I-AA.

Thankfully, Dooley and Papp gave us a final insight for that, too.

When asked how they would go about accumulating the necessary information to decide the future of KSU football, both Dooley and Papp offered a list of schools they would look to for guidance, and a possible blueprint. Dooley mentioned South Alabama, Texas-San Antonio and Lamar. Papp talked about Old Dominion, Georgia Southern and Georgia State. Five of the six currently play in the FCS and four will remain there permanently—only South Alabama and Texas-San Antonio have their sights set on an FBS future.

In nine months, September 2010, Dooley and his committee will make a recommendation to Papp whether to move forward with KSU football, and all the report will say is what we already know.

In the fall of 2013, the Owls will be the newest FCS program. The only question left is whether Dooley can convince Georgia to come to Kennesaw for the inaugural home opener.

BLANKENSHIP'S DAD MAKES MESS OF AN UNFORTUNATE SITUATION, JANUARY 7, 2017

It is hard to be on the right side and the wrong side of an issue at the same time, but that is where the family of former Sprayberry High School standout and current Georgia kicker Rodrigo Blankenship are today.

Earlier this week, Ken Blankenship, Rodrigo's father, made it clear about the want and need for his son to be put on scholarship. Blankenship sent out an 18-paragraph statement to the media outlets around the state saying the fact Rodrigo was not put on scholarship after the season was "an injustice to him as well as a crushing hardship for his family."

Here is where the family is on the right side of the argument.

Rodrigo has earned his spot and should have been put on scholarship.

For the season, he went 14-of-18 on field goals with a long of 49 yards and made all 26 of his extra points. He earned SEC Special Teams Player of the Week after going 4-for-4 on field goals, including the game-winner as time expired against Kentucky, and then grabbed a spot on the SEC All-Freshman team.

In addition to his great improvement over the course of the season, Rodrigo also became somewhat of a cult figure, thanks to his quirky glasses and interview style of answering questions with his helmet on. His popularity also garnered the catchphrase, "Respect the specs."

Like most families that send their kids to college, Ken Blankenship is right about the cost. It can become a strain on their financial situation. If he would have only left his statement there, this wouldn't have become a big story.

Only he didn't, and this is where he ends up on the wrong side.

In his statement, Blankenship called out coach Kirby Smart. He gave detailed information about a private meeting he, his son and the coach had about the scholarship situation. He complained about the way Smart was prepared to defend the decision why Rodrigo would not be put on scholarship until at least the end of the school year.

Then, worst of all, Blankenship questioned Smart's loyalty to his son.

"Why is (Rodrigo) remaining at a school where the head coach refuses to acknowledge that his contributions are more than worthy of being on scholarship?"

Unfortunately, this isn't the first time Blankenship has questioned Smart's loyalty or honor. Blankenship did it right after the Kentucky game, in an email to the DawgNation website.

"Rodrigo has committed to the 'G,' but we are puzzled why Coach

Smart has not yet committed to the 'R,'. His support seems to stop at the front gate of the scholarship house."

If Blankenship is trying to back Smart into a corner, it's not going to end well.

Let's remember who Smart worked for the previous nine years—Alabama head coach Nick Saban.

Smart has already adopted many of Saban's policies as his own, and wants as quickly as possible to be coaching for a national championship, like the Crimson Tide will be Monday night.

One of Saban's biggest traits is he doesn't put up with distractions. He made that perfectly clear this week when he told offensive coordinator Lane Kiffin, who had accepted the head-coaching position at Florida Atlantic but intended to remain with the Tide for the remainder of their playoff run, to leave seven days before the biggest game of the season.

If Saban is willing to do that, and Smart has taken those teachings to heart, how difficult will it be for him to wash his hands of the Blankenships?

Now, out of difficult situations, character is formed and revealed. The night Ken Blankenship's statement made news, Rodrigo Blankenship released his own on his Twitter feed. It said the following:

"Dear Bulldog Nation,

"It is of the opinion of many of you that my performance this season has justified that I be placed on scholarship. It is of the opinion of many of you that my performance this season failed to justify a scholarship. My opinion of whether or not I feel a scholarship is warranted is rather irrelevant; therefore I will not voice my opinion on the matter.

"Georgia deserves the best players it can possibly find at every position, and in order for this program to regain the national notoriety and respect that it so rightfully deserves, the program demands production for each and every position that is nothing short of impeccable. It is evident Georgia deserved better than what I was able to offer this season, and I would like to apologize for my clearly-defined deficiencies.

"I would also like to apologize for my father's interactions with the media this season. He acted without my knowledge each time, and each incident was uncalled for."

Rodrigo Blankenship has taken the high road. It appears he understands his situation, whether he agrees with it or not.

Based on Rodrigo's statement, it also appears that Smart may have found himself a leader.

It takes some internal fortitude to call out a family member for their indiscretions, especially if it is your own father. If nothing else, maybe Rodrigo's statement will help Ken Blankenship pause for self-reflection before releasing another.

Editor's note: Ken Blankenship is a former sports correspondent for the Marietta Daily Journal.

THEY KNOW 'BO': BOHANNON HIMSELF, AND THOSE CLOSEST TO HIM, FEEL KSU COACH HAD 'DESIRE TO BE A WINNER', MARCH 27, 2013

Brian Bohannon grew up around football, and from his middle-school days on, he had a short list of things he wanted to accomplish.

Those who know him best say he accomplished them all through hard work.

Bohannon was so sure of his projected path in life, he wrote a report about his life's ambition in the seventh grade that his mother kept.

"It is my desire to be a winner," he wrote. "I want to play football, and be a football coach."

At age 42, the Griffin native and Woodstock resident has already gone beyond his simple list. As of Sunday, he was no longer just a football coach—he was the first head coach in Kennesaw State history.

"I grew up on a football field," Bohannon said during his introductory news conference Tuesday inside the football locker room at Fifth Third Bank Stadium. "I had a lot of conversations (with my dad). He's been a rock."

His father, Lloyd, was the longtime coach at Griffin High School, compiling a career record of 156-58-1 from 1978-95. As a youngster, Brian would go with his father to practice after school, eventually playing for him from 1986-89.

"I was just around it every day," Brian Bohannon said. "When I was young, that was my time with him. You can't help but absorb things. You learn how to handle people and what it took to be successful."

His father wasn't so sure.

"I don't know if I taught him anything (about being a coach)," said Lloyd Bohannon, who still lives in Griffin, "but he had a lot of characteristics to be a good coach. He was a very hard worker and he always had the respect of his teammates."

That respect grew as Brian Bohannon's workload did. And it was the hard work he put in as a wide receiver at Griffin that caught the eye of Georgia coach Ray Goff.

Brian Bohannon's senior year at Griffin was Goff's first as the Bulldogs' head coach, and it caught the family off-guard when Goff wanted to bring Bohannon to Athens.

"(Brian) was a good player," Lloyd Bohannon said, "but he wasn't a big-time recruit. It was a surprise when Goff took interest."

Bohannon arrived on the Georgia campus in 1990 and was among the first receivers who benefitted from the more open passing offense Goff employed when Marietta native Eric Zeier arrived on campus the following year.

Early on, however, Bohannon's roommate, Chad Wilson, almost didn't allow it to happen.

Wilson, who eventually played wide receiver and defensive back for the Bulldogs, was recruited to Athens as a quarterback. Bohannon found out the hard way that his roommate was out of position.

"I threw him a pass during practice," said Wilson, now a senior vice president with First National Bankers Bank, "and with his good hands, you knew he was going to catch it. But I led him a little too far, and the defensive back just laid him out.

"Instead of getting upset, he just got up, came back to the huddle, and said, 'Make sure you make a little better pass next time.'"

As a competitor, it could have been a time for Bohannon to confront his roommate for leading him astray. Instead, Bohannon said it was times like those that were teaching moments for both a coach and a player.

"You have to know the personality of your team," he said. "They are going to feed off me. There are going to be times that players get upset and lose their temper, but that's OK."

Wilson said that particular play showed the kind of true competitor Bohannon really was.

"What is he — 5-foot-11, 170 pounds and ran a 4.8 40? What is he doing as a wide receiver?" Wilson said. "The dude is competitive. He'd catch anything."

It was all about the work ethic Bohannon learned growing up in Griffin.

"I had to work hard," he said. "I wasn't talented enough not to. If I didn't do the work, I wasn't going to get a chance to play."

The competitive nature didn't end on the football field. It carried over to the softball diamond.

"Intramural softball," Wilson said. "He'd still be going all out. Even there, he was as competitive as I've ever seen."

"I think he's going to be a perfect fit for (the KSU) job."

Once Zeier got there, Bohannon became an integral part of the offense.

"Any time you play at Georgia, you are really good at what you do," Zeier said. "You have to be when you are playing with guys that are going on to play in the NFL, like Andre Hastings and Arthur Marshall."

Bohannon went on to letter all four years at Georgia. He started his junior and senior seasons and was part of the 1992 team that won 10 games, tied for the Southeastern Conference's Eastern Division championship and won the Citrus Bowl.

Zeier remembers one play that signified Bohannon's career as a player, and now his style as a coach.

"We ran a quick out one time, a 12-yard out," Zeier said. "I don't remember who it was against, but he caught it and took it in for a touchdown. I had to throw the ball so early, so he had to run the perfect route or he wouldn't catch it. It was because of his meticulous attention to detail that he ran exactly the right route at exactly the right depth.

"He is meticulous and detail-oriented across the board."

It was during that 1992 season that Bohannon's list of goals from his seventh grade report came back to the forefront.

At the suggestion of his mother, Carol, he was on a path toward earning a business degree, but the closer he got to graduation, the idea of the business world became less appealing.

"My junior year, I thought about things I could do with that degree," Bohannon said. "I think, at that time, I already knew I was going to be a football coach."

Bohannon did complete the business degree and went on to West Georgia to earn a master's degree in business education. But while he was doing that, he was working as a graduate assistant coach.

"I would go over to West Georgia to watch practice," Lloyd Bohannon said. "I would sit in the bleachers and talk about the merits of coaching college football with (former Georgia defensive coordinator) Richard Bell.

"I would talk about (Brian) coaching in college and Richard would say, 'He should go coach in high school.'"

At the time, the conversation seemed to make sense. Lloyd Bohannon was about to retire from Griffin, and Brian may have had an opportunity to coach at his alma mater, but Lloyd said it was never discussed.

Brian Bohannon left West Georgia when he got his first full-time coaching job as the wide receivers coach at Gardner-Webb, but his stay there was a short one. The following year, he was hired by Paul Johnson at Georgia Southern.

"We went 62-10 at Georgia Southern (from 1997-2001)," Bohannon said. "We won two national championships and played for a third.

"One day, he comes in and says, 'I have this opportunity to go somewhere,' and he asked, 'Do you want to go with me?' And I said yes."

In 2002, Johnson and Bohannon landed at the Naval Academy, a place that puts order above everything else. It was the perfect spot for a trait Wilson said he and his college roommate both had.

"We were both neat freaks in McWhorter Hall," Wilson said of the old athletic dorm at Georgia. "Brian and I were always very organized. I may have been a little more OCD than he was, but it is something that has served him well."

Six years later, Johnson—and Bohannon—had another opportunity. This one was to come back to Georgia—not to coach the Bulldogs, but to go to their archrival, Georgia Tech.

"I asked him, how he could do that to his kids," Wilson said jokingly. "He said, 'That's OK, we're Jackets now!'"

Now, Bohannon's family—wife Melanie and children Blake, Braden and Brooke Anna—are Owls.

Bohannon said he has spent 17 great years with Johnson, and there were many other people who helped him to get where he is. His longtime mentor was happy that Bohannon was able to become Kennesaw State's first coach and offered him some advice as he embarks on his new challenge.

"He said, 'Be who you are,'" Bohannon said. "He's been unbelievably good to me. I owe a lot to coach Johnson."

OVERCOMING EARLY JITTERS, MASON WINS FOR BULLDOGS, DECEMBER 1, 2013

ATLANTA—For Georgia, the Hutson Mason era officially arrived with 1:43 left in the second quarter at Georgia Tech's Bobby Dodd Stadium.

Before then, many Bulldog fans were probably thinking Mason's time behind center should end before it had a chance to begin.

"I'm sure they were," said the former Lassiter star, who completed 22 of 36 passes for 299 yards, two touchdowns and an interception in his first college start. "I didn't play very well in the first half. But all we needed was that one touchdown."

That one touchdown came after Mason entered the huddle down 20-0, just looking for an opportunity to make something happen.

What happened was he started trusting his teammates as much as they trusted him. What it led to was seven straight scoring drives and a 41-34 victory over Georgia Tech in double overtime. It also brought to an end a very long week for the redshirt junior from east Cobb.

After Aaron Murray suffered a torn anterior cruciate ligament against Kentucky last week, Mason was thrust into the role of starting quarterback. For the first time since arriving in Athens in the spring of 2010, he was "The Guy."

Now, it was Mason doing all the interview requests, taking all the reps in practice. And now, all the eyes of Bulldog Nation were on him.

Considering it had been more than four years since he started a game, the week proved to be all he could handle.

"It was nerve-wracking," Mason said. "I didn't sleep well all week. I wasn't getting to bed until 1 or 2 a.m. Last night, I went to bed at 9:30 p.m. just to make sure I got some rest."

It looked like Mason had gotten plenty of sleep during pregame warmups. Every throw was on target and he hit his receivers between the numbers.

But it didn't translate to the game.

Mason chalked that up to first-start jitters, and his angst with watching Georgia Tech continue to pick up key third downs to keep the clock running.

"Getting down 20-0 against that offense — every time they pick up a first down, it's 5 minutes they take off the clock."

Former Georgia All-American and Marietta High quarterback Eric Zeier said earlier this week that it would take two drives for the nerves to subside. It actually took four, but when Mason got in the huddle with 1:43 to play before halftime, he finally settled down. And when he did, Mason looked like the record-setting quarterback he was at Lassiter, and the SEC quarterback he always wanted to be.

Mason started the drive with a 13-yard completion to running back Todd Gurley. He followed with 17- and 22-yarders to wide receiver Chris Conley, and a 10-yarder to J.J. Green out of the backfield. Four straight completions moved the ball from the Georgia 14 to the Tech 24 with 42 seconds left.

After Mason tucked the ball and went around the left side for 16 yards on a scramble, he calmly hit Gurley for a 10-yard touchdown.

Seven plays, 86 yards, and Georgia was back in the game.

Before that drive, Mason was 4-of-8 for 44 yards and the interception. After, he went 18-of-28 for 254 yards, two touchdowns, and he completed every must-have throw he attempted.

On the first drive of the second half, he completed a back-shoulder throw to tight end Arthur Lynch for a 30-yard gain on third-and-10. It helped set up a field goal.

A 33-yarder over the middle to Conley on the next drive led to a touchdown and pulled Georgia within 20-17.

Mason said that was his biggest throw of the game to that point.

"If he doesn't make that catch, we may not win," he said.

It was definitely true the next time the Bulldogs got the ball. Trailing 27-17, Mason found himself faced with fourth-and-6 from his own 39.

With his poor start to the game now a distant memory, Mason connected with Michael Bennett for 11 yards and a first down.

"It was good for Hutson," Georgia coach Mark Richt said. "He was patient, and I think the guys trust him. This win is going to help settle him down. When he looks back at the film, he's going to see some things he'll think he should have done differently, but it gives you an idea of what could happen in the future."

The only thing missing from Mason's second-half performance was the game-winning touchdown pass, but that was only because he didn't get a chance to throw one.

In overtime, Mason told the offensive line that Gurley was set to break loose.

"Let's just get a hat on somebody," he said.

It took four running plays in overtime for Gurley to run 50 yards and score two touchdowns. The second — on the first play of the second overtime — was one where Mason may have wished he kept the ball himself.

"My grandma with a cane could have run through that hole," Mason said.

Georgia Tech still had a chance to force a third overtime, but after the Yellow Jackets' final pass hit the ground, and Mason knew Georgia had won the game, he took a moment for himself. He wasn't among the many Bulldogs that rushed the field, but it didn't take long for the emotion to come to the front.

After a few high-fives and hugs with teammates and coaches, Mason climbed to the top of the Redcoat bandleader's platform and looked for his parents in the crowd. He never found them, but what he did see was Bulldog Nation staring back at him, and he liked what he saw.

"This is what it's all about," Mason said. "All those times when I thought about transferring and sitting and talking with coach Richt—this game, this is the type of game I dreamed of. This was the kind of game I dreamed about being part of. I'm so thankful for this opportunity, and I'm just glad to be a Bulldog."

On Saturday, the Bulldogs were happy he was, too.

PANU'S 15 MINUTES: WHITEFIELD GRAD EARNS SCHOLARSHIP, WHIRLWIND TWO WEEKS IN SPOTLIGHT, AUGUST 12, 2012

Forgive Vanderbilt's Marc Panu if he has to stop and take a breath, because it is unusual for a backup fullback to get the kind of attention he has gotten the last two weeks.

Panu, a 6-foot-1, 240 pound former Class A First-Team All-State defensive end at Whitefield Academy, was given a full scholarship worth more than $50,000 August 8, by Commodores coach James Franklin. The fact that a fourth-year walk-on player earned a scholarship is not out of the ordinary, but the moment was recorded and then posted on the Vanderbilt website and YouTube. The video went viral registering more than 355,000 views to date, and for Panu, it has all been a bit overwhelming.

"It's hard to explain," said Panu, who has a 3.8 grade point average and is on track to graduate with a degree in Chemical Engineering next year. "I've tried not to let it be a distraction (for the team)."

In this case, it's been a good distraction.

After being posted on the Vanderbilt website, Panu's story gradually has gotten bigger and bigger. There have been stories by the Associated Press, blogs were written about him on ESPN.com, most of the other sports websites linked to his video, and last Friday, Panu and Franklin were interviewed on Fox and Friends.

"I'm trying not to let it get to me," said Panu, who has seen most of his previous action on the punt and kickoff units on special teams. "Everyone gets their 15 minutes of fame."

Franklin has been hailed as a great, young, up-and-coming coach that is changing the recruiting culture at Vanderbilt. He is a player's coach and his surprising Panu with a scholarship is another way of proving himself. As Panu found out, it's also a way of getting a former walk-on's full attention.

"I had no idea it was coming," Panu said. "Because he will often do stuff like that."

The stuff was putting a highlight reel of Panu's practice performance on the big screen in the team meeting room and showing the team exactly the kind of effort he expects out of each of his players.

"You want to watch a guy who is trying to find a role on this team?" Franklin asked. "A guy that keeps his mouth shut and loves being part of this team."

Video rolls of three devastating blocks Panu put on defenders during practice, including a pancake block that springs a running back for a touchdown.

It was after that when Franklin announced to the team that Panu had earned his scholarship. It was an announcement that stunned Panu, knocking him back in his chair, and brought his teammates to their feet for a standing ovation.

"I was really in shock," he said. "It was really a blessing."

It was also a shock to his parents.

"We heard from him during a time he is normally in meetings or at practice," Marc's mother Judith Panu said.

She added that as soon as she heard the news, the tears began flowing.

"We were excited," Marc's father Al Panu said. "It was a sense of rejoicing that after working for over four years that he would get a scholarship."

The Panu's said Marc had earned some academic scholarships and had to take out some loans, in addition to the financial help from the family. But while Judith Panu said it did "stretch" their finances, the celebration was about Marc's perseverance and not so much about the financial break.

"We just appreciate the recognition from coach Franklin, (offensive coordinator and running back coach John) Donovan and his teammates for reacting the way they did."

Franklin told Fox and Friends the decision to give Panu the scholarship was a "no-brainer."

"It's about giving people opportunities and Marc's done a tremendous job for us," Franklin said. "It's the perfect example of—have a positive attitude, have tremendous work ethic, and good things will happen to you."

A positive attitude and work ethic are things Panu said have carried him this far, and maybe a little luck to go with it.

"I have no idea why this (attention) has happened to me over anybody else," Panu said. "Walk-ons all over the country earn scholarships. But hard work is the key. And luck is where opportunity and preparation meet."

COULD-BE BULLDOG A PROUD COWBOY,
SEPTEMBER 5, 2009

The University of Georgia may be about to learn the hard way a lesson my father taught me at an early age.

You don't know what you have until it's gone.

That may be the case when Bulldogs coach Mark Richt looks across the field today at Oklahoma State's Boone Pickens Stadium and sees No. 30 dressed in burnt orange, white and black, knowing that if he had offered David Paulsen a scholarship a little earlier, the former Walton Raider would be starting his season dressed in Georgia red and black.

From the time Paulsen moved to Marietta from Florida when he was 8 years old, he was a fan of the Bulldogs. And, as he grew and began to realize he would be able to compete at the highest level of college football, Paulsen wanted to run out onto the field at Sanford Stadium wearing a helmet emblazoned with the Georgia "G."

Unfortunately, a different color got in the way.

"Georgia was a finalist (to sign David)," according to Paulsen's father, Kirk, speaking on behalf of his son, who isn't allowed to speak to the media because of Oklahoma State's rule against freshmen being interviewed by the media. "Coach Richt and (offensive line and running game) coach (Stacy Searles) were in our home one evening for dinner and were offering David a grey shirt."

Student-athletes are allowed five calendar years to play four seasons. A grey shirt means that particular player delays his entrance into school until what would normally be the spring semester of his freshman year. By waiting until the spring to start college, a player would be playing his final season in the sixth year after high school rather than the fifth.

Kirk Paulsen said no player that Richt has ever grey-shirted, including David Pollack, amongst others, had not been awarded a scholarship during the spring semester.

That would have been fine for the younger Paulsen, who had gone to all the Georgia football camps and had gone to every one of the Bulldogs' home games the last few years.

That is, if Oklahoma State coach Mike Gundy hadn't entered the picture.

Gundy is best known to college football fans from a rant a couple of years ago when he yelled during a press conference, "I'm a man! I'm 40!" The coach's tirade came as he was sticking up for one of his players, which David Paulsen said was one of the reasons he considered the Cowboys in the first place.

But, at the same time that Richt and Co. wanted David to wait a year, Gundy was always telling him he was the main guy Oklahoma State wanted.

"We had dinner with coach Gundy," Kirk Paulsen said. "That night, he kept telling David that he was their No. 1 choice, their top pick for fullback, and was the player at the top of their board."

David Paulsen was sold. Despite his love for the University of Georgia, he was going to be a Cowboy.

But the story doesn't end there.

At 6:42 a.m. on National Signing Day last February, David got a phone call. He didn't answer, but recognized the phone number with the 706 area code as coming from the University of Georgia. By 7 a.m., David had signed his college scholarship papers with Oklahoma State.

When he went to listen to the voicemail from Georgia, David was surprised to hear it was from Richt himself.

As Kirk Paulsen recollected, the message went something like this: "David, this is coach Richt. I probably should have done this a long time ago, but I'd like to offer you a scholarship to the University of Georgia."

Too little, too late.

Since then the Paulsens have had the time-consuming task of de-Georgia-fyng their house, changing the decor to emphasize their new

Halloweenish orange-and-black color scheme with pride. The only thing they have left is a picture of David with Richt that still hangs on the refrigerator.

Kirk Paulsen said the irony of David's first college game being against Georgia has not been lost on his son, the rest of his family or his friends, who have given David a lot of good-natured needling.

Even strangers have gotten into the act.

"I was wearing my OSU shirt going through Hartsfield Airport," Kirk Paulsen said. "Georgia fans stopped me and said, 'Just wait until we play you.'"

Well, the wait is almost over.

The proud parents, Kirk and Tammy Paulsen, were scheduled to head to Stillwater, Oklahoma, on Friday.

David, who turned 19 earlier this week, enters today's game listed as the backup fullback on the Cowboys' depth chart and should also see time on the special team units.

But according to Kirk, his son, at 6-foot-3 and almost 250 pounds, could also be used as the short-yardage battering ram when the Cowboys need a yard, which would make this an interesting scenario:

Six seconds to play, Georgia up six with Oklahoma State facing fourth-and-goal from the Bulldogs' 1 and David Paulsen's number is called.

"I think Tammy and I would have a heart attack," Kirk Paulsen said.

Maybe Richt will, too, knowing what might have been.

DOOLEY A GOOD SPORT FOR A GOOD CAUSE, AUGUST 11, 2009

Vince Dooley knows how to take a joke.

He also knows how to take a compliment.

Dooley graciously got plenty of both Saturday as some of the University of Georgia's biggest football heroes took their turns at the microphone at the Vince Dooley Roast and Tribute at the Renaissance Waverly Hotel at the Cobb Galleria Centre with the proceeds going to the Aflac Cancer Center at Children's Healthcare of Atlanta.

One by one his former players — Kevin Butler, Lindsay Scott, Frank Ros, Ray Goff, Bill Stanfill and others, along with dignified guests — including the First Lady of Georgia football, Barbara Dooley, Bill Hartman from WSB Channel 2 in Atlanta and longtime sideline reporter Loran Smith — took their best shots late into the night to the delight of the over 1,000 UGA fans in attendance.

The lone down note of the evening may have been that Hershel Walker, the Bulldogs' record setting runner, Heisman Trophy winner and freshman leader of Dooley's 1980 national championship team could not be there because his plane was stuck on the tarmac in Dallas. But even that was made into a lighter note by WSB's master of ceremonies Neil 'Hondo' Williamson told the audience there was already a precedent of being able to have fun without him when he quipped, "We went 10-1-1 without him in 1983."

Throughout the evening there were the recurring themes of how Dooley was able to give and save.

The first was how every member of the Georgia nation has benefited by Dooley's 40-year affiliation with the university, first as coach and then as athletic director from the lessons he taught and the opportunities he provided.

The second was Dooley's perceived love of money and the idea he may still have the first dollar he ever earned after becoming coach in 1963.

Butler, the Bulldogs' kicking legend who beat Clemson with a SEC-record 60-yard field goal in 1984, and then won a Super Bowl as a member of the 1985 Chicago Bears, took the first shot.

"Some people call him cheap," he said about his former coach. "Cheap doesn't sound too nice. Frugal is a better word. But, I can tell you he's never pulled a hamstring reaching for his wallet to pick up a dinner check."

Smith recalled one time when he and coach traveled to South Georgia to play in a golf tournament. Smith was unaware he was expected to attend a dinner function following his round. After the tournament he went into town to purchase the necessary clothing for the evening.

"I told the shopkeeper, 'I'm looking for something cheap in a men's suit,'" Smith said. "The shopkeeper looked over my shoulder and said you're in luck, here comes Vince Dooley."

Dooley himself got into the act during his rebuttal of the evening's comments when talking about the current Bulldogs' coach.

"If there is one person that has a chance to be at one place a long time (like I was) it's Mark Richt," he said. "And I want to be his financial advisor."

But in the end, it was Barbara Dooley who put her husband's ability to save a dollar in perspective when she decided to have a conversation with the women in the audience.

"Vince has all the same flaws that other husbands have. He doesn't listen to his wife," Barbara said.

Now 45 years into their marriage, Barbara explained how Dooley, for years, had a difficult time remembering her birthday, mainly because it fell in the middle of two-a-day fall practices. So after being in the doghouse for many years Dooley finally told her, "Give me a week's notice and I will never forget your birthday again."

The following year came and Barbara, sitting at the breakfast table while Dooley is engrossed in that day's sports section, tells her husband the following Thursday is her birthday.

She got no response.

"Again, I told him, 'you told me to tell you a week ahead of time, and I am telling you my birthday is next Thursday.'

"The paper never moved.

"At this point I know he's not listening to me when he finally shrugs and says, 'What do you want?' I thought to myself I'll show him and said, 'I want a divorce.'

"After a moment he finally looked out from behind the paper and said, 'I didn't plan on spending that much money.'"

OWLS FIND IDENTITY, CONTINUE TO RUN THROUGH DEFENSES, NOVEMBER 5, 2017

A trip to the dentist's office.

That's what I thought of while watching Kennesaw State run the football against Montana State on Saturday afternoon.

The Owls masterfully found a way to beat the Bobcats 16-14 in snowy, cold Bozeman, Montana, using short, quick-hit type runs that had to feel like a dentist continuing to pick and drill in and around an ever deepening cavity, and not allowing the patient enough time to rinse.

Three yards here. Five yards there. Pick up four more on fourth-and-2. Pick, pick, whirrrrrrrr.

Kennesaw State did it from the opening kickoff to the final whistle. Pick, pick, whirrrrrrrr.

The Owls ran the ball 74 times for 346 yards, and they capped off their performance with a final drive that will become the standard in what it means to run the triple-option at KSU. Starting from the 2 yard line, the Owls went 78 yards in 20 plays and took 10:03 off the clock. They continued to extend the drive by converting on two third downs, two fourth downs and added another first down on an offside penalty. By the time Justin Thompson lined up for what proved to be the game-winning 37-yard field goal, the Montana State defense had to feel like they were getting a root canal without Novocain.

"I told the guys we had to score on that drive," coach Brian Bohannon said. "They found a way. It wasn't pretty, but they found a way."

While the last drive allowed Kennesaw State to win its eighth game in a row and improve its record to 8-1, it was all the 3-, 4- and 5-yard runs before it that made it possible.

The Owls had four 10-play drives or longer. They took the opening drive of the game 17 plays for 89 yards and took 8:27 off clock. It ended with Chandler Burks going in from 2-yards out through a hole big enough for a snow plow to drive through.

They followed that with an 11-play, 62-yard drive just before the half for Thompson's first of three field goals, and then in the third quarter, KSU went 16 plays for 47 yards. It didn't result in points, but it took 7:11 off the clock. After the defense forced a punt just 1:46 later, the offensive line had the Bobcats right where it wanted, and it went out and imposed its will.

The Owls finished the game with an advantage in time of possession of 39:32 to 20:28. That was magnified in the fourth quarter where they controlled the ball for 12:35, and an astounding 18:30 of the final 21 minutes of the game.

Of course, the best part of this game going forward wasn't that they beat Montana State this way, it was they had to beat the Bobcats this way. For the first time in the three-years of the program, Kennesaw State was all but shut down on the edges. Montana State was able to string plays out, force the runners back inside and not allow the big plays that can happen when the Owls get in rhythm. They won this game between the tackles when there was no other choice. Burks ran 34 times for 149 yards. Jake McKenzie picked up his third 100-yard game in the last four weeks by carrying the ball 20 times for 116 yards.

McKenzie had the longest run of the game—a 30 yarder up the middle. Only once did it seem like KSU found the edge, when Darnell

Holland took a pitch for 21 yards. Despite that, the team averaged 4.7 yards a rush.

Saturday's game was the farthest Kennesaw State has traveled in its short history and the 23 degrees at kickoff was 31 degrees colder than any previous Owls football game on record. Now, they get to come back to balmy Georgia to close the regular season with two home games—next Saturday against Charleston Southern (5-4, 2-1 in Big South) and the following week against surprising Monmouth (8-1, 3-0).

With the win over traditional power Montana State, which had already knocked off then No. 17 North Dakota and narrowly lost to two other ranked teams this season—No. 10 South Dakota State, No. 11 Eastern Washington—the Owls know their game can go anywhere, play in any element against any opponent.

The nice thing is they won't have to go far, and if the running game continues to practice dentistry at the highest levels in front of the home fans, the Owls will finish its root canal on the Big South—and cap it with a big, shiny crown.

IN MIDST OF HISTORIC SEASON, KENNESAW STATE FOOTBALL TEAM TRIES TO KEEP THINGS LIGHT ON SIDELINE, NOVEMBER 8, 2017

KENNESAW—Kennesaw State's football team is finding more ways to have fun.

Just look at the sideline.

Sure, there are still high-fives and fist-bumps, but if you look closely now, Plank and the barber shop are there, too.

During the Owls' 16-14 win at Montana State last Saturday, both activities were front and center in the final moments of the game.

Plank is a block of wood from the Cartoon Network series "Ed, Edd and Eddy." Plank is an imaginary friend that randomly seems to move about, and lately it has been presented to a special teams or defensive player who makes a big play, gets a big hit or forces a turnover.

When former Kell High School standout Taylor Henkle intercepted a pass late in the fourth quarter to all but seal Kennesaw State's win, he was presented with Plank—with its crudely drawn eyes and smile—on the sideline.

The only problem was, he wasn't really sure why.

"I've seen it around the locker room and in people's lockers, but I didn't ask any questions," Henkle said. "I don't know who came up with the idea to hand it to me after the pick. I didn't know what to do with it, so I held it up, and there were a few Kennesaw State fans there in the front row, and they took the picture.

"Hopefully, it gets tossed around a lot on Saturday."

Kennesaw State (8-1, 3-0 Big South Conference) will host Charleston Southern on Saturday, with a win keeping the Owls in the driver's seat for the conference championship and automatic bid to the national tournament.

While Henkle may not have known all the ins and outs about Plank, Kennesaw State coach Brian Bohannon did some homework to find out about the wooden award.

Bohannon said former Kennesaw Mountain standout Tanner Jones, a scout-team receiver, found Plank on spring break, and over the last few weeks, began bringing it to the locker room. Just like the cartoon, Plank gradually found its way from the locker room to the sideline, and then to the bench.

"One of our players took the plank out to the bench for the Gardner-Webb game," Bohannon said. "I think the plank just kind of hangs out on the sideline, sits on the bench and drinks juice. I don't know."

"The plank is like a person—like, during the game Saturday, the plank had a snowcap on, because it's cold out."

Bottom line, winning is fun.

"It just adds a little something to the celebration of making a big play," Henkle said. "You have to remember to move on to the next play, but little things like that make it a little extra fun."

Once Henkle put Plank down, it was time for celebration No. 2.

"If you make a big play, or make a touchdown, it's off to the barber shop," he said.

There, defensive lineman Desmond Johnson is in charge as the primary stylist.

"He does a good job," Henkle said.

Other members of the team assist. Someone offers a hot towel, another holds the mirror while a third brushes off any imaginary hair. Anyone can help, but its Johnson's shop.

"(Defensive lineman) Barclay (Miller) was trying to clean up my beard," Henkle said, "but it was a little rough. I told him to take it easy because I like it."

Would Henkle see Miller or Johnson when in need of a real shave or a haircut?

"Absolutely not," he said.

The players and coaches know this could be a special season, and they have their heads on straight. Everyone is focused, but not too wound up, to make some memories along the way.

"The bottom line is, our kids are having fun," Bohannon said. "You are supposed to go out and compete and play hard, but it's supposed to be fun. I want them to enjoy it and have fun, as long as it's in the right way."

COBB DUO LEADING UAB INTO THE SWAMP, SEPTEMBER 7, 2011

Greg Franklin grew up a Georgia fan.

Now, he's about to do something no current Bulldog has done — or will ever do — and that's start against Florida at the Swamp.

The former Marietta High School standout, will be the starting tailback when UAB opens its season Saturday night in front of 90,000 Gator fans in Gainesville.

"I'm looking forward to it," said Franklin, a sophomore who rushed for 53 yards in limited playing time for the Blazers in 2010. "I'm looking forward to playing in front of a big crowd. I may be a little nervous at first, but after the first snap it should go away."

Franklin can say that because of past experience. During his freshman season, he played on special teams the first three games of the season. But, when he got his first chance to line up at running back, Franklin was playing in the only stadium in the SEC that makes the Swamp look small — Tennessee's 102,000 seat Neyland Stadium.

Now consider the case of Franklin's UAB teammate, and fellow Cobb County product, Kennard Backman.

The former Whitefield Academy standout will be making his college debut as the Blazers' starting tight end — as a true freshman.

A year ago, Backman was opening his season against Walker, on Whitefield's cozy home field. This year, he'll be kicking off the season at Florida, where he'll likely be eye-to-eye with preseason All-SEC linebacker Jon Bostic or 6-foot-4, 295-pound defensive end Sharrif Floyd.

No offense to the Walker School, but I don't think they have too many kids on their campus the size of Floyd.

Welcome to college football, Kennard.

It's enough to make his head spin.

"College football is totally different," Backman said. It's almost like a different sport. You can't rely on your physical ability. In high school, you could get away with things because you were bigger, faster or stronger. Now everybody is like that.

"But I never thought, three or four years (after first taking up football at Whitefield), that I would be lining up against Florida."

In fact, five years ago, Backman would have never thought about playing football—period. He was a basketball player when he arrived at Whitefield Academy, but as he grew into what has become his 6-4, 235-pound frame, football coach Jimmy Fields convinced Backman he had talent that could translate to the gridiron.

And even though he's folded up his basketball shorts, that doesn't mean Backman's totally abandoning his former sport.

"I think it's helped with my footwork and stamina," he said. "You have to use your feet to guard and block and the stamina has helped with my routes."

Good feet will only help Backman so much in Gainesville, but he got a little extra advice from two of his former Whitefield teammates now in the collegiate ranks—Vanderbilt defensive end Marc Panu and Wake Forest defensive end Kris Redding.

"They talked about how much more serious football is at this level," Backman said, "because it's a job coming out with the hard hat every day."

One person that thinks Backman is ready is Franklin. Not only has Backman's work in camp vaulted him to the top of the depth chart, but also the sense of bravado and confidence he exudes.

"He stood out (in fall camp) with his ability to catch the ball," Franklin said.

"I was in the huddle (last week) and asked him, 'Are you ready? What are you going to do? Are you nervous?' He said, 'I'm not nervous.'"

Backman played his entire football career in front of 500 to 1,500 people, but don't think he won't have jitters or butterflies in his stomach about what waits for him in four days.

"Well, I'm not nervous—yet," he said.

Starting from the get-go, Backman is now expected to hold on to his job for the next four years.

Franklin, on the other hand, will be trying to earn more playing time for his. He is currently filling in as the starting tailback because UAB's leading rusher from last season, Pat Shed, is down for a few weeks with a sports hernia.

Ironically, it was an injury—a broken ankle—suffered by Franklin in the Cobb Senior Bowl following the 2009 season that might have kept him from grabbing the starting spot during his freshman year. But now that he's completely healthy, Franklin says he's ready to go.

"Last year, I was just trying to get used to the plays," he said. "But I'm ready for it. I feel comfortable now, and my ankle is 100 percent."

In addition, the once small-framed Franklin has gotten bigger (bulking up from 172 to 190 pounds) and faster (dropping his time in the 40-yard sprint from the high 4.4-second range to the low 4.4s).

With those kinds of numbers, it's hard to believe Franklin isn't playing in the ACC or SEC—he had offers from N.C. State, Vanderbilt, Kentucky and Georgia before deciding on the Blazers. But after his injury, some schools began to back off.

Not UAB.

"I felt like they wanted me," Franklin said on signing day in the winter of 2010.

Now, he gets to prove that he would have been playing in the country's largest stadiums.

And it's a fair bet that Saturday many of the Georgia fans—who hate anything orange and blue—will be rooting for he, Backman and the Blazers, too.

GEORGIA HELPED SET JENNINGS IN MOTION, OCTOBER 5, 2014

WellStar CEO Reynold Jennings made the right choice. In 1964, he was at the University of Georgia, as a member of the "Bullpups"—then the freshman football team.

That first year, he learned that playing SEC football as a 5-foot-9, 160-pound defensive back may not be the best plan for him.

"It was the Georgia Tech game," he said. "I prided myself on my tackling on the kick-coverage teams. I was always the first guy down the field. Well, I was in position to make the tackle and the Tech receiver did one of those fake-left, fake-right, and then he ran right by me.

"When you see those guys on the field, they are different from us."

On the field is exactly where Jennings was last Saturday. He was part of a halftime reunion at Sanford Stadium, celebrating the 50th anniversary of legendary Bulldog coach Vince Dooley's first team.

"It was really nice," he said. "All the members of the '64 team were on the sidelines. When we went onto the field, we stretched from the 25-yard line to the 25-yard line. They played a tribute video on the Jumbotron and then the key varsity players spoke. It was very emotional."

The reunion allowed Jennings to catch up with some of his former teammates. They told stories and talked about the antics that went on in the dorms.

The 68-year-old Jennings also saw some of the lifelong ailments his friends had been inflicted with, thanks to the game they all loved.

He was happy he went into the medical field.

"I never second-guess," Jennings said. "I have no regrets."

But that didn't mean he completely gave up the game on his own free will. He had help.

Jennings came back for spring practice in 1965. He had gained 15 pounds and could run the 100-yard dash in 10 seconds, but in one of the blocking drills, Jennings had to go up against Louis Sutera, a 230-pound fullback from Atlanta.

Sutera lettered for Georgia in 1965 before entering the U.S. Army, ascending to the rank of sergeant and serving as a forward observer doing reconnaissance work.

Sutera was killed in action in 1967, trying to save the lives of some of his men.

"I went to block him, and all I saw was stars for about 5 seconds," Jennings said. "Well, I wasn't going to let him get the best of me, so I got in there again. I went to block him, and again, all I saw was stars."

Something else happened.

Sutera's hit drove Jennings' facemask and helmet back into his nose and forehead. The doctors told him that his nose was not broken, but many of the blood vessels in his face had been severely damaged.

The injury drove Jennings straight to Georgia's pharmacy school.

"I realized I'm not big enough to hang on here," he said.

Jennings graduated from Georgia in 1969 and went on to the University of South Carolina, where he received a master's degree in business administration.

Even as he entered business, the Dalton native always returned to the lessons he learned on the football field as the ones that helped shape his professional career.

"You toughen up and become a man," Jennings said. "You build confidence and learn to overcome adversity."

The latter point was driven home in high school.

Growing up in Dalton, Jennings was playing his senior season at the high school and preparing to play a Cedartown team coached by "Doc" Ayers—who went on to become Jennings' freshman coach at Georgia—in the region championship game.

The game was scheduled for Nov. 22, 1963.

That afternoon, President John F. Kennedy was assassinated in Dallas.

Jennings and the team knew the game wasn't going to be played that night and they were dismissed by their coaches.

There was only one problem. Without cell phones and email, communication was limited in north Georgia, and Cedartown was already on the road.

"The players got called about an hour before the game, and we were told it was back on," Jennings said. "We just had to try to adjust our mindsets."

Cedartown went on to win the game 7-2. Two weeks later, it beat North Clayton for the state championship.

"We felt really bad," Jennings said, referring to the sadness of the loss and the president's death.

Football helped Jennings decide where he was going to go to college. A good athlete, there were a number of schools interested in him coming to play on scholarship.

Initially, Jennings chose Middle Tennessee State University, but a talk with his high school coach, Bill Chappell, set him straight.

"He told me, 'You need to go where you have the broadest academic possibilities,'" Jennings said.

From that conversation, he knew he would be going to Athens.

Jennings also relishes the relationships he was able to make because of football. Edgar Chandler was his teammate at Dalton and went with him to Georgia. Chandler was a three-year letterman and defensive captain before playing for the Buffalo Bills.

While at Georgia, Jennings got to know future Pro Football Hall of Famer Jake Scott and defensive captain and three-time letterman Tony Lawhorne, who went on to become a vascular surgeon in Macon.

Jennings also calls former teammates Don Cope, the CEO of Dalton Utilities, and Bill Sampson, the former superintendent of Cook County Schools, as close friends.

While he never played in a varsity game for the Bulldogs, Jennings knows he did the next best thing.

"I got to play my games in Sanford Stadium under the lights on Thursday nights," he said. "People used to sit on the railroad tracks and watch us.

"It's true today as it was back then. When a team signs 25 players a year to scholarships, only about 15 of the 25 guys last all four years. So, I'm one of the few who can say I played between the hedges. Then, I got to watch my friends play. Like I said, no regrets."

FOR MASON, LUTZENKIRCHEN, BOND BRIDGED SEC RIVALRIES, JULY 4, 2014

Sunday morning, Hutson Mason woke up to a text message from Zach Mettenberger, who was briefly Mason's teammate at Georgia.

That's not out of the ordinary. Mason keeps in touch and has had many conversations with Mettenberger over the last few seasons, even as Mettenberger went on to play at LSU and, most recently, was drafted by the Tennessee Titans.

But that wasn't all.

Mason's former coach at Lassiter High School, Chip Lindsey, had also called.

At that point, Mason knew and felt that something was wrong.

It was then that he learned that Philip Lutzenkirchen, his friend since age 7 and teammate with the Trojans' basketball and football teams, had died in a one-vehicle accident that also claimed the life of Joseph Ian Davis, just after 3 a.m. near LaGrange.

Since then, there have been numerous outpourings of emotion and celebration of the 23-year-old Lutzenkirchen's much-too-short life.

On Sunday, the Auburn faithful rolled Toomer's Corner one more time to pay tribute. More than 1,000 people came to pay their respects

Wednesday night during a memorial at Lassiter's Frank Fillmann Stadium, and what seemed to be an equally large crowd turned up to Thursday's funeral Mass at Transfiguration Catholic Church in east Cobb, forcing police officers on site to create parking spaces on the fly.

While all those people had a connection to Lutzenkirchen, very few, if any, had the relationship Mason kept with the person who arguably became the best tight end in Auburn history. And Mason was one of the last people who had an opportunity to talk to Lutzenkirchen—less than 48 hours before he died.

"It's a conversation I'll cherish," said Mason, Georgia's expected starting quarterback for the 2014 season. "It seemed like it was God-ordained. He reached out to me and said he was praying for me. He wanted me to have a big year this season after all the things I went through (waiting four years for the chance to start).

"I was lucky Friday to have that conversation. I'm counting my blessings. I just wish I had a superpower where I could go back and tell him not to get in that car."

After the accident, Mason got together with many of his former high school teammates and, as is often the case, they began to tell stories. He said they talked about Lutzenkirchen's quick wit and sense of humor.

But while there were many practical jokes played within the group during their high school years, Mason said the one that always seemed to come to mind was the simplest, and it involved him, Lutzenkirchen and former Lassiter defensive back Brad Penter. It ended with Mason usually getting in trouble.

"Philip would always put gum in Brad's hair and blame me," Mason said. "And then he'd just smile."

Of course, when football players are in a room, inevitably the talk turns to the game.

"We all laughed about how bad we were," Mason said.

Unfortunately, Mason was right. During his freshman and sopho-more seasons, Lassiter could do no better than a 3-7 record.

But that all changed when Chip Lindsey brought his wide-open spread offense to the east Cobb school, and what it did was unleash the talents of both Lutzenkirchen and Mason.

In 2007, Lutzenkirchen caught 42 passes for 494 yards and seven touchdowns. It was enough to earn a scholarship offer from Auburn, but it was nothing compared to what was to happen in 2008.

"I knew Philip was my best target," Mason said. "We always had the non-verbal communication. All it took was a nod or a wink."

In 2008, Mason threw for 3,705 yards and 27 touchdowns. Seven-ty-three passes, 1,000 yards and six touchdowns went to Lutzenkirchen, who became a nightmare for opposing coaches and players to try to de-fend.

"We had (wide receiver) Marlon Anthony, who was tall but thin," Kell coach Derek Cook said. "But Philip was the same height and could do so much more because of his size. We didn't have anyone that could match up with him."

Rocky Hidalgo went one step further.

"He had size, speed and agility," said the former Walton coach now at Glynn Academy. "He was the size of a power forward."

Lutzenkirchen used those basketball skills to introduce himself to the world late in the 2008 season in a game against Centennial.

On fourth-and-7 from the 12-yard line, Mason found Lutzenkirch-en guarded in the back of the end zone. Trying to take advantage of Lut-zenkirchen's height, then listed at 6-foot-4, Mason threw high, allowing his tight end to make a play.

The ball, however, was too high. Instead, Lutzenkrichen went up, caught it, and with momentum of the throw taking him out of bounds, he batted it back in play to Reid Handler for a touchdown.

"Hutson threw it up and, when I realized I wasn't going to be in (bounds), I pushed it to Reid," Lutzenkirchen said at the time. "The Centennial players just kind of waited around and didn't go for the ball, because they saw it was going long. Reid and I were still trying to make a play because it was fourth down."

The play was featured on ESPN's SportsCenter and continues to live on in YouTube infamy.

That season ended with Lassiter winning nine games, including one in the state playoffs for the first time in program history. Mason was named the Class AAAAA Offensive Player of the Year, and Lutzenkirchen was the first-team all-state tight end.

It was that kind of effort that endeared Lutzenkirchen to the Auburn faithful.

Of course, a 2010 game-winning touchdown catch against Alabama in the Iron Bowl, during the Tigers' national championship season, didn't hurt either. His touchdown dance — the "Lutzie," a high-stepping shimmy-shake — still brings smiles to Tiger fans around the country.

However, once Lutzenkirchen arrived at Auburn, he didn't forget about his high school quarterback. Despite his breakout season, Mason had not been highly recruited going into his senior year, but his soon-to-be college rival made sure that would change.

"Philip really helped me with the recruiting process," said Mason, who threw for 4,560 yards and 54 touchdowns his senior season, setting every single-season passing record in the state's record books. "Once he was done (with recruiting), he got me in touch with all his recruiting contacts. He helped me get my highlight tapes and my name out there.

"He really was the older brother I never had."

Now, Mason has a void. His big brother is gone, but he will never be forgotten.

At this point, Mason is unsure how best to honor Lutzenkirchen for everything he meant to him.

Knowing both men, it seems like that question may be easy to answer. All Mason has to do is the best he possibly can.

It's the way Lutzenkirchen approached every game.

However, I bet Lutzenkirchen wouldn't mind if Mason borrows the "Lutzie" after throwing a game-winning touchdown pass for Georgia in an SEC or national championship game.

DRAKE TAKES INJURIES, UNDERSTUDY STATUS IN STRIDE, GOES OUT WITH HIGHLIGHT-REEL TD, JANUARY 12, 2016

Hello, world. I'm Kenyan Drake.

Of course, that's not actually how the former Hillgrove High School star introduced himself to the rest of the football-watching population outside SEC country. Instead, everybody knows his name today because he fielded a kickoff, started upfield, cut toward the left sideline and went 95 yards for a touchdown, with the last 5 yards caught on pylon cam that made it look like the 6-foot-1, 210-pound running back was diving into your lap.

It was the last time Drake would touch the ball as a college football player, and it was the biggest play of his Alabama career.

"I knew I was running out of gas," Drake said Tuesday morning on ABC's "Good Morning America." "I knew I had a defender on my tail closing in, so I just wanted to give my last-ditch effort and dive for the end zone, and luckily it worked out for the better."

While there were plenty of other big plays in the Crimson Tide's 45-40 victory against Clemson, it was Drake's return that essentially put the game away, and it's why he's on the front cover of Sports Illustrated this week.

In addition to SI, Drake graced the front page of the sports sections of the Chicago Tribune, Orlando Sentinel, Knoxville News Sentinel, Tampa Bay Times and Arizona Republic on Tuesday.

Not bad for a kid from Powder Springs, Georgia—population 14,411.

"That's going to be a special memory for Kenyan. That kickoff return was really something special," Alabama coach Nick Saban told the Tuscaloosa News.

It's also special considering some of the things Drake, who set a championship game record with five kick returns for 196 yards, had to overcome during his four years in Tuscaloosa.

He arrived on campus as part of Alabama's heralded recruiting class of 2012, which included wide receiver Amari Cooper, defensive back Landon Collins, linebacker Reggie Ragland and fellow running back T.J. Yeldon.

Thanks to a number of injuries that beset the Crimson Tide's backfield, Yeldon found himself as the primary backup to Eddie Lacy that fall, and Drake moved into the No. 3 spot, where he ran for 281 yards—and earned a national championship ring—as a true freshman.

After running for 694 yards and eight touchdowns as a sophomore, it looked as if Drake may have been set up for a breakout season as a junior in 2014. He scored three touchdowns in a win against Southern Miss, then had a career-long 87-yard touchdown catch against Florida the following week. But instead of being able to continue building on his momentum, a broken leg against Ole Miss ended Drake's season.

The injury situation got no better this fall. Drake suffered a broken rib against Ole Miss, sprained an ankle and suffered a concussion against LSU, then broke his arm against Mississippi State.

It was an injury that required surgery and could have ended Drake's college career. He has a long scar across his right forearm that will likely remain for the rest of his life as a reminder, but he only missed two games.

Drake ran for 409 yards this season, finishing his career with 1,495 rushing yards and 18 touchdowns. He also caught 46 passes for 570 yards, which will be a big selling point as he prepares for the next part of his career — the NFL.

Despite being a backup all four seasons — to Lacy, Yeldon and this year's Heisman Trophy winner, Derrick Henry — Drake is considered by many experts to be a potential second-day selection in this April's draft, probably because you can't teach 4.3-second speed in the 40.

As a senior at Hillgrove in 2011, Drake could do just about anything he wanted on the football field. Before the season, he told me he had only one goal.

"I want to be the best player (on the field)," he said.

Drake ran for more than 1,600 yards and was named Georgia's Gatorade Football Player of the Year. Every game he played in, he was the best player on the field.

For 99.9 percent of his college career, Drake didn't have the opportunity to reach that lofty goal. With 7:47 left in the fourth quarter Monday night, all that changed, and for 16 seconds — the time it took him to from one end of the field to the other — he was the best player on the field, in the biggest college football game of the year.

Not a bad way to make an entrance into the public consciousness.

Not a bad way to call it a college career.

BURKS' CAREER COMES TO AN UNCEREMONIOUS END, DECEMBER 8, 2018

KENNESAW — This was not the way "Captain Touchdown" was supposed to end his career.

With 10:57 left in the second quarter and Kennesaw State trailing 10-3, quarterback Chandler Burks was on one knee, 15 yards behind the line of scrimmage, and wincing in pain.

The graduate student, who was the program's first verbal commitment and its first signee, and who helped lead the Owls to nearly unprecedented success in just the fourth year of the program, was out of the game.

"He got hit on the funny bone, but it wasn't real funny," Kennesaw State coach Brian Bohannon said after losing 27-17 to South Dakota State in Saturday's Football Championship Subdivision quarterfinal at Fifth Third Bank Stadium.

Burks said he got hit around the elbow area. He said it was where all the nerves seem to come together, and the injury would not let him extend his arm to pitch the ball—a key in the Owls' triple-option offense.

Despite that, Burks kept trying to get his arm to respond.

For much of the third quarter, he held a ball in his left hand while roaming the sideline. He worked with center C.J. Collins on taking snaps, and he kept trying to extend and pitch the ball. He even tried to talk his coach into letting him back on the field.

"He tried one time," Bohannon said, "but I talked to the trainer and was told he just couldn't extend his arm completely. Maybe if he would have had a little longer to work on it, he could have made it.

"He's the starting quarterback for a reason. I would have loved to have been able to put him back in. We just couldn't do it."

It was an unceremonious end to a career that deserved a much better sendoff.

Burks finished his final season with 1,043 passing yards and 10 touchdowns, but he will be remembered for what he did on the ground. The Walter Payton Award finalist ran for 905 yards and a single-season FCS quarterback record of 29 rushing touchdowns.

For his career, Burks ran for 3,431 yards and 56 touchdowns and last year became the first quarterback in Big South Conference history to run and throw for 1,000 yards in the same season. The 56 touchdowns are an all-time Big South record for any position, and Burks finished as the conference's all-time leader in scoring. He also helped Kennesaw State to a 37-12 record through four seasons.

When Burks arrived on campus for his first season—the first year of the program when all the team did was practice—he tore an ACL. Instead of falling behind in the pecking order, he did everything possible to make sure he was ready if and when his name was called.

By the middle of his redshirt sophomore year, Burks was ready.

Burks took over after Trey White got hurt in the opening half of the 2016 season opener against East Tennessee State, and Burks never looked back.

He dealt with the bumps and bruises that come with being an option quarterback. Just like Saturday, there were times that Daniel David came in to relieve him, but Burks was always ready to play the next week, so it was odd for everyone—fans, coaches and teammates—to see him standing on the sideline in the biggest game of his career.

Of course, the one surprised the most was Burks himself.

"It sucked," he said. "It sucked not to be able to go out there and play with my brothers."

And knowing the competitor inside, Burks found a way to show one final act of leadership. He became a sounding board for David and helped him in any way he could, because he knew it was all he had left.

"At that point, if I would have gone back in the game, it would have done more harm than good," Burks said.

There will be more postseason accolades.

Burks has already been named the Big South Offensive Player of the Year for a second time. He will likely be named an All-American, and he will attend the FCS awards banquet in Frisco, Texas, on the night before the national championship game to see if he wins the Payton Award as the best offensive player in the FCS.

Any awards Burks gets will be nice and well-deserved, but that won't take the sting off of what happened on Saturday.

Win or lose, he deserved to be on the field with his teammates, but, just like the game, some things don't work out the way we hope they will.

FORMER MCEACHERN STANDOUT TREMAYNE ANCHRUM RELISHES SECOND NATIONAL CHAMPIONSHIP AT CLEMSON, JANUARY 9, 2019

Tremayne Anchrum is a two-time national champion.

As a member of the Clemson offensive line, the former McEachern High School standout played a key role in the Tigers' 44-16 victory over Alabama on Monday in the College Football Playoff national championship game in Santa Clara, California.

This time, however, it was much sweeter than the first.

The 6-foot-2, 310-pound junior left tackle earned a championship ring as a freshman when Clemson won a title to end the 2016 season, but he only played about 15 to 20 snaps per game. This time, Anchrum was a starter and helped keep true freshman quarterback Trevor Lawrence upright and sack-free.

"When you are a key contributor, there is a lot of pressure," Anchrum said, "but I've played in a lot of big games. I played in a lot of big games in high school at McEachern, and it really helps you prepare."

Anchrum and his linemates allowed Lawrence to complete 20 of 32 passes against Alabama for 347 yards and three touchdowns. They also opened holes for running back Travis Etienne, who scored two touchdowns and ran for 86 yards on only 14 carries.

It was the kind of performance every team hopes to have, but many cannot provide.

Anchrum was not shy in the enthusiasm he had for the game's postscript. He said the Tigers did exactly what they had game-planned, and while most would not have expected Clemson to win the game by four touchdowns, Anchrum was not completely surprised by the margin of victory.

"We expected something like that," he said. "We had a plan for whatever they wanted to try to do. We didn't have a plan to win the game. We had a plan to dominate."

Anchrum said much of the feeling came from the preparation in the week of practice leading to the game, but he credited coach Dabo Swinney's pregame speech—and an assist from Rocky Balboa—to getting the team pumped up.

"I'll remember the beginning of the game," Anchrum said. "They were playing 'Eye of the Tiger' (from Rocky III) as we came out. It was really corny, but it really got us going."

What also got the team going was a 44-yard interception return for a touchdown by Clemson's A.J. Terrell less than 2 minutes into the game. Anchrum said he could tell at that point that Alabama was worried.

"That first pick-6, they knew we weren't afraid of them, and you could see it in their eyes," Anchrum said.

When Clemson beat Alabama for the championship two years ago, it did so with a touchdown pass with 1 second to play. Anchrum said he and his teammates knew Monday night that there would be no need for any late-game heroics after Alabama tried to run a fake field goal early in the third quarter.

"Any time you go for it on fourth down, it's a statement," Anchrum said. "We didn't really expect them to run the fake, but we said, let's line up that way just in case. When they ran it, we knew we had won the game right there because they were panicking."

The only thing Anchrum was not expecting Monday was the reaction Clemson's victory would bring. He said, normally, he hears from family and a few friends after a win.

Not this time.

"I heard from everybody," Anchrum said. "I started hearing from people I haven't heard from in years."

Some of the most rewarding messages came from his McEachern family. He said athletic director Jimmy Dorsey sent him a congratulatory text message, with Dorsey saying "I knew you were a champion when you first got here."

Anchrum also said he heard from many of his former teammates.

"Those are my guys and always will be," he said.

Anchrum is starting his final semester of school this spring and is on track to graduate with a business degree, but he also knows he has a year of eligibility remaining. He said a master's degree could be in the works, and he also knows another solid season could propel him into the NFL.

Right now, though, Anchrum said he is going to take a breath and enjoy this moment for a while.

"It's crazy. To go 15-0, that is so special," Anchrum said. "We beat a great Alabama team that was supposed to be the best college team in history. It feels good."

OWLS PUTTING THEMSELVES IN BLUEPRINT DISCUSSION, OCTOBER 5, 2019

When people think of the gold standard when it comes to start-up football programs at the Football Championship Subdivison level, most will focus on one program—Georgia Southern.

For the first 32 years of the program that was reborn in 1982 following a post-World War II dormancy, the Eagles won six national championships in a tradition started by former Georgia defensive coordinator Erk Russell and later continued by Paul Johnson.

There have been a flurry of programs that have been born since 2000.

Of those, most who follow FCS football say Old Dominion is the program to be used as a blueprint.

If you take a close look, there is a third team that could be wedging itself into the discussion of how to do it—Kennesaw State.

When the Owls defeated Missouri State two weeks ago, it marked the 40th win in the program's short program history. It took only 53 games to get there.

That is better than every program that has started since the year 2000, with the exception of Old Dominion, which did it in 52 games.

In the short four-plus years of the program, Kennesaw State has never been under .500, has a record of 24-4 at home and has an even more absurd record of 36-1 when leading after the third quarter.

When reviewing the other teams that began football since 2000, very few come close to Kennesaw State's production.

Mercer started its program two years before the Owls, and the Bears were looking to win their 40th game in their 75th attempt. East Tennessee State, which relaunched its program the same year Kennesaw State kicked off for the first time, is looking for win No. 22.

Looking back to the announcement of football coming to Kennesaw back in 2010, it would be hard-pressed to find anyone who would have believed this amount of success could be achieved this fast—including coach Brian Bohannon and then-athletic director Vaughn Williams.

However, both agree the program has successfully followed the vision they had in getting it started.

"I think we've been pretty close," Bohannon said. "The goals we put in place were long-term. We put everything in place for long-term success. Now, there have been some things we've had to navigate along the way, but the things we wanted to do, the way we wanted to look, the way we wanted to go about our business, I think we had a good plan. We have to give our kids and coaches credit to get them to win enough, to get enough buy-in the way we do things to have carry over from class to class."

That buy-in started in 2013, shortly after Kennesaw State hired Bohannon from Johnson's staff at Georgia Tech.

Bohannon and his assistants had to sell players on creating history. They had to sell them on creating a foundation for future success to be built upon. Williams said it took a special ability to convince players in an instant-gratification society to come to campus and be patient, and he credited Bohannon and the staff for pulling it off.

"There were the aspirations, desires and hopes that we would be able to build something like this," said Williams, now the senior associate athletic director at Boston College. "Now, when I look back, I sit back and smile. Bohannon has done a lot of work, and the players got behind that vision."

When Bohannon and Williams created the vision, they had one huge advantage going for them—the university was in the state of Georgia.

Talent is abundant, especially in and around the metro-Atlanta area. Both men knew it was a built-in recruiting advantage, and if done right, they wouldn't have to go far to create a roster that would be able to compete in any league around the country.

That has remained the case. Of the 100 players on the Owls' 2019 roster, 78 of them are from Georgia, and all but three are from the Southeast.

As play began in 2015, it was important for Kennesaw State to have a means to develop rivalries, so getting into the Big South Conference starting on Day 1 was key. Players immediately had a chance to play for something. That has paid off with two conference championships already, and two automatic bids into the FCS playoffs.

In addition, while there always seems to be some controversy about it, the triple-option—or, at least, Bohannon's modified version of it—has allowed the team to be successful faster than it might have been. The running game has been the calling card of the Owls, who lead the country in rushing with 369.8 yards per game this season and have never finished outside the top six in the FCS since they started playing.

While fans may wish the team threw the ball more, or ran a flashier offense, it is hard to argue with results. It also begs the question, would you rather win like Kennesaw State, or throw the ball all over the field and finish 5-7?

"I have conversations with other athletic directors up here," Williams said. "I don't understand why more (unestablished) programs don't want to try the triple-option. Teams don't want to have to prepare for something they don't see every week. It gives you an advantage."

One other thing Bohannon and the staff have done is schedule accordingly.

It was important to build a winning tradition early, especially at home. Initially, that was why teams like Point, Shorter and Clark Atlanta found their way onto the schedule.

With Kennesaw State's continued success since, those games are trying to disappear, but now it is going in the other direction. There aren't as many teams that are willing to agree to play the Owls prior to the postseason because teams in other conferences may not be able to absorb another loss and remain a viable playoff option.

"We leveraged relationships," Williams said. "We got games wherever we could get games."

Going forward, scheduling will be a big challenge, and not just with non-conference games.

Currently, the Big South is down. Heading into Saturday's games, the conference's teams had a combined overall record of 16-22. Only Kennesaw State, Campbell and Hampton had winning records, which puts more pressure on each non-conference game to be able to make a statement to the NCAA selection committee.

However, it's hard to want it any other way. Currently, the Owls are becoming a victim of their own success. They even have a better record than Georgia Southern did when they got their 40th win. However, the Eagles did win national championships in Years 4 and 5.

Kennesaw State hasn't gotten there yet, but it is knocking on the door. It is all part of Bohannon's vision of long-term success, and at this point, it's hard to doubt that it will eventually happen.

SUGAR BOWL SHOWS FIELDS' TRANSFER DECISION HAS BEEN MADE, JANUARY 2, 2019

If there was ever a question on whether Justin Fields was transferring from the University of Georgia, Tuesday night's Sugar Bowl gave us the answer.

Fields is gone.

The freshman quarterback and former Harrison High School star stood on the sidelines with his helmet on for four quarters. Despite participating in all the practices, and from what all the reports told us, he was locked in and prepared to help the team if called on, Fields never moved.

Once the game was over, and the media was allowed in the locker room following the 20-minute cool-down period, it was reported that the 6-foot-3, 225-pound signal caller was nowhere to be found.

During the game's broadcast on ESPN, play-by-play man Sean McDonough said something that stood out. He said that Georgia coach Kirby Smart had told Fields the coaching staff wanted him to stay in Athens. Smart was said to have told Fields, "If you transfer, you'll have to sit out anyway, so why not redshirt here?"

It has been reported Fields is trying to get an NCAA hardship waiver because of an incident that happened during a game in October. A Georgia baseball player was said to have hurled racial slurs at Fields while he was on the sidelines. To do so, Fields and his family were expected to retain attorney Tom Mars, who helped former Mississippi and current Michigan quarterback Shea Patterson get a waiver last season.

To make his statement, Smart must not think Fields, who threw for 328 yards and four touchdowns, and ran for 266 yards and four more scores in limited action this season, will get the waiver. Regardless, if the coaching staff really wanted him to stay, it passed on a golden chance to prove it.

For much of the first three quarters of the Bulldogs' 28-21 loss to Texas, the offense sputtered. Quarterback Jake Fromm continued to miss wide open receivers, and skill position players like running back D'Andre Swift and wideout Jeremiah Holloman looked uninterested.

Fields could have had his Tua Tagovailoa-moment, by coming off the bench and potentially giving the offense a spark. But unlike Tagovailoa, who was put in the game after halftime and led Alabama's second-half comeback in last year's national championship game against Georgia, Fields wasn't given an opportunity. He didn't even get the usual packages the coaches installed for him during the regular season.

That likely means one of two things. Fields went to Smart and the coaching staff and told them he was definitely leaving, or, the coaching staff was saying, thanks for your time here, but don't let the door hit you on the backside as you leave.

Either way, it doesn't point to having Fields back between the hedges next season.

So, what happens now? Ohio State still seems like the eventual landing spot.

Buckeyes' quarterback Dwayne Haskins said before the Rose Bowl that Fields had reached out to him to find out what he was going to do.

Haskins has said that he is 50/50 on whether he will return to Ohio State or enter the NFL Draft, but don't buy into that, he's gone, too.

The redshirt sophomore is coming off the best season in Big Ten history. He threw for 4,831 yards, 50 touchdowns, and just eight interceptions while completing 70 percent of his passes.

Haskins has been given a first-round grade by the NFL's College Advisory Committee. He's likely to be selected in the top 10, where the New York Giants (No. 6) and Jacksonville Jaguars (No. 7) will both be in the market for a quarterback, and last year's first-round projection for the No. 6 selection was a four-year deal worth $24.3 million.

You can always go back to college, but that kind of money doesn't come around that often. He has to make his decision by Jan. 15.

For Fields, the Buckeyes appear to be a good fit. New head coach Ryan Day is a former quarterback that has worked as a QB coach in college and the NFL. While Haskins wasn't asked to run much, Day's offensive scheme is perfect for a dual-threat quarterback. In 2017, Day helped J.T. Barrett throw for 3,053 yards with 35 touchdowns and nine interceptions. He also ran for 798 yards and 12 scores.

With Fields' size, strength and throwing accuracy, he would be a combination of the best of Haskins and Barrett.

Other places that Fields is expected to consider are Oklahoma, who have had back-to-back Heisman Trophy winners in Baker Mayfield and Kyler Murray, and Florida State.

It's too bad things have not worked out for Fields at Georgia. It would have been fun to see a Cobb County native lead the Bulldogs to a potential national championship.

Now, it looks like he'll be another player in a long line that tries to prevent it.

BLANKENSHIP HAS EARNED HIS ACCOLADES, NOVEMBER 24, 2019

I started hearing about Rodrigo Blankenship during his freshman season at Walton in 2011.

There were stories about his powerful leg. Things that shouldn't be possible for someone that, at the time, looked like he was about 50 pounds soaking wet. I finally got to see him in person the following year after he had transferred to Sprayberry.

The Yellow Jackets were playing Pope on a Thursday night and it allowed me to sneak out of the office to cover a game. It turned out to be a defensive battle that the Greyhounds won 14-12, but as people filed out of the stadium, the only topic of conversation was of Blankenship and a missed game-winning field goal attempt. But this wasn't just any miss.

With 1 minute left in the game, Sprayberry drove to the Pope 45-yard line and Jackets' coach Billy Shackelford called time out. When the team trotted back onto the field an audible gasp and some chuckles could be heard from the Pope fans near the press box because Shackelford was about to let his sophomore kicker attempt a 60-yard field goal. About that time, Pope coach Matt Kemper used a time out of his own. He knew.

"That kid is dangerous," Kemper said after the game.

Knowing that any kick that was going to go 60 yards was likely to be driven off low, Kemper put every tall player he could find to try and block Blankenship's attempt. It didn't work.

When Blankenship's toe met leather it sounded like someone had shot off a cannon. The ball cleared the line and was heading straight down the middle. It just needed to fly another foot. Instead of clearing the crossbar, it smacked it flush. The ball rebounded off the crossbar and flew back to the 40 yard line.

"We were 3 inches from a victory," said Shackelford, who had routinely seen Blankenship make 61- and 62-yard kicks in practice. "There aren't a lot of NFL kickers that could have tried that one."

Players on both teams looked stunned.

"Wow, unbelievable," one player said. "That kid has a cannon for a leg," said another.

From that point, the legend of "Hot Rod," was born.

Saturday, the scrawny kid from Sprayberry with the thick glasses became Georgia's all-time leading scorer. With four field goals, Blankenship passed Blair Walsh for the all-time lead with 418 points. He has at least two games to pad his new mark—and if the Bulldogs take care of business, it could be as many as four. He will finish as the SEC's second leading scorer in conference history.

Blankenship is a success story. A former walk-on, he was eventually put on scholarship and became a leader of the special teams. Last December, he graduated cum laude from the Grady College of Journalism and Mass Communication, with a degree in digital and broadcast journalism, completing his path a semester early.

Last week, Blankenship was named a finalist for the Burlsworth Trophy, which is awarded to the most outstanding college football player in America who began his career as a walk on. He is a national semifinalist for the Lou Groza Award, which goes to the nation's best kicker, he could be the SEC Special Teams Player of the Year, and an All-American.

He has forged his spot into Georgia's record books, and into the hearts of Bulldogs' fans all over.

Next stop is a long and distinguished career in the NFL.

"Respect the specs." He's earned it.

KENNESAW STATE DESERVES BETTER FANS,
DECEMBER 5, 2018

The Kennesaw State fan base embarrassed itself on a national level last Saturday.

The feeble crowd that came to Fifth Third Bank Stadium to see the Owls beat Wofford in the second round of the Football Championship Subdivision playoffs would not have filled any of the small Class A high school stadiums in Cobb County.

The announced paid attendance was 3,515. The actual number of spectators may have been half that. It was by far the smallest crowd in program history.

This is for a team that in four years of existence has won two Big South Conference championships and is making its second trip to the FCS quarterfinals. It has won 24 of its last 26 games, and 15 straight at home.

Of the eight playoff games played last weekend, only South Dakota State, which is based in the major metropolitan area of Brookings, S.D., population 22,056, drew a smaller announced crowd. The Jackrabbits played Duquesne in a snow storm, 30 mph winds and drew 3,042.

The other six games averaged 8,660.

Sure, the weather wasn't perfect, but it's December in Georgia. There was rain, but the temperature still reached the mid-50s. Yes, Georgia was playing for the SEC championship, but not until two hours later.

Football is an emotional sport. Teams feed off the energy of the crowd, but you left your team hanging. There was no energy in "the Nest." No noise and few cheers, but there was a whole lot of apathy.

Knowing the conditions weren't great, the athletic department went out of its way to try to get people to the game. It offered a free tailgate where fans could get free food and drinks before the game.

It also gave free admission to the first 1,000 students. Yet, at kickoff, not counting the band, there were 60 students in the stands — the number was so small it was easy to count. By the end of the first quarter, it may have increased to 150, and didn't get any bigger.

Unfortunately, this lack of attendance isn't a one time thing.

The program opened four years ago with a crowd of 9,506 against Edward Waters. Fifth Third Bank Stadium hasn't seen a crowd nearly that large since. The inaugural season drew an average paid attendance of 8,820. It has dwindled to 6,175 this season, with most of the actual crowds in the 4,500 range.

How is it the team goes 6-5 in Year 1, 8-3 in Year 2, 12-2 in Year 3 and now 11-1 in Year 4, yet the average crowd size per game continues to get smaller?

It makes me wonder if the third largest university in Georgia deserves a football team, let alone the No. 2 team in the country.

That's especially true for the students. You are in class with these players. They are your friends, and you have a chance to tell people that you were a fan from the beginning. You have had a chance to be there when the inaugural signing class built the foundation for what could eventually be a championship program.

The team averages 45.7 points per game, is 22-3 all-time at home and has one of the three best players in the country in Chandler Burks, who was made a finalist for the Walter Payton Award — the FCS version of the Heisman Trophy — on Monday.

Instead, you are letting that chance slide by.

The same can be said for the alumni and the surrounding Kennesaw and Cobb County community. Sure, the majority of people said they wanted football at KSU when the exploratory committee first proposed bringing the sport to campus. It would be nice if all those that helped bring it here now backed it up by showing up at the games.

On Saturday, Kennesaw State is going to host South Dakota State with a chance to advance to the FCS final four. The Jackrabbits are from the Missouri Valley Conference, which is considered to be the best in FCS, and it is their third straight trip to the quarterfinals.

It's the kind of game where a big crowd and a rowdy student section could make a big difference. The athletic department is again doing its part by letting the first 1,000 students in free.

Unless North Dakota State is upset, which is unlikely, this will not only be the final home game of the season, but the final home game for Burks, Darnell Holland, McKenzie Billingslea, Anthony Gore, C.J. Collins, Justin Sumpter and the other seniors that have represented your program so well.

They deserve to be sent off in front of a full house. Too bad you don't care enough to make it happen.

BASKETBALL

DULUTH—McEachern won the Class AAAAA girls state basketball championship Friday.

If there's any justice, Monday, the Lady Indians should be the national champions.

McEachern came into the state title game ranked No. 2 by ESPN and No. 3 by USA Today, but after its 33-point victory over Hillgrove, the Lady Indians did more than enough on the court to jump Phoenix's St. Mary's Catholic High School for the No. 1 spot.

"We are 33-0. We have six girls going to Division I schools. We deserve it," McEachern coach Phyllis Arthur said. "In my eyes, we're national champions."

The Lady Indians should be national champions because they reacted like national champions do when pressure is applied.

After McEachern built a 21-point lead early in the third quarter, Hillgrove cut the deficit to 12 entering the fourth. The game could have gone any way at that point, but Pachiyaanna Roberts and Dominique Wilson would not let it happen.

They combined to score 10 of the next 12 points, the lead was extended to 22 and the Lady Indians' party was on.

All that's left to celebrate is the possibility of a national title, but according to ESPN, the Lady Indians could have won the game by 333 points and it wouldn't have made a difference. The titles are going to St. Mary's.

The big question is, why?

St. Mary's is a good basketball team. It finished its season 30-0 with its own state title, but put them side by side with the Lady Indians and McEachern has better than just an argument.

McEachern and St. Mary's have each beaten five teams in the current ESPN top 50. But that's where the latter's case ends and the former's begins.

St. Mary's won the prestigious Nike Tournament of Champions, a tournament held in December that brought 16 of the best high school teams together as a college showcase. But the tournament was held in Chandler, Ariz., just a few miles from St. Mary's campus, making every game it played—including those top-50 games against Riverdale Baptist (Md.), Good Counsel (Md.) and Cicero-North Syracuse (N.Y.)—a virtual home game.

When McEachern played its tournaments against the nationally ranked opponents, the Lady Indians started on the road.

They beat Memphis Central and Overton (Tenn.) across the state line in the Tennessee Turkey Jam. The Lady Indians then followed by beating Hoover (Ala.) and Riverdale (Tenn.) in the Jump Off Holiday Invitational a bit closer to home at Holy Innocents' Episcopal School in Sandy Springs.

But the biggest argument in favor of the Lady Indians is that they beat ranked teams when the pressure was the greatest.

At no time was there another team from Arizona ranked in the top 50, which means St. Mary's didn't have to face one in its state tournament. McEachern went and beat Norcross in the Lady Blue Devils' gym to begin the season, and they did it again Thursday night in the state semifinals.

Hillgrove kept the Lady Indians from a chance to play North Gwinnett, which was ranked, in Friday's championship game. But, by making it an all-Powder Springs final, the Lady Hawks — they should have been ranked, too — have a good chance in supplanting North Gwinnett in the final national poll.

Hillgrove's only losses this year came to McEachern (four times) and Lovett, which will play for the Class AA state championship today. If the Lady Hawks get the nod, that would mean, in the end, McEachern will have won nine games against top-50 squads — including two in the final four to win the title. Seven of those wins came away from Lovinggood Gym.

Unfortunately, there's only one way to truly settle the argument, and it's not going to happen.

"I want to play them so bad," Roberts said, "Because you can't really determine who's No. 1 unless you play them."

Arthur said she's willing to have her team suit up, and there are 15 newly crowned state champions in her locker room that are ready for the challenge.

Cobb County's national champions against Phoenix's.

Hey, St. Mary's, you ready?

What time is tip-off?

GHSA: BASKETS IN WRONG POSITIONS, MARCH 6, 2016

If any of the players and coaches who participated in this week's Georgia High School Association basketball state championship games thought the basket seemed farther away than normal, it was.

Ernie Yarbrough, the GHSA's coordinator of basketball, confirmed to the Marietta Daily Journal that the stanchions that support the baskets were placed roughly 1 foot farther back from where they are supposed to be.

Yarbrough went on to say that the GHSA was made aware of the issue Saturday afternoon, but because the tournament was already behind schedule, there were no plans to fix it. He said it would take about an hour to move the stanchions into the proper place.

Yarbrough said the court was prepared by officials from the Macon Coliseum, where the games are being held. The 15 state championship games—including one for wheelchair athletes—are among the few basketball games held inside the 48-year-old arena.

Allatoona boys coach Markus Hood alerted officials to the problem Friday night, before the Buccaneers took the floor for the Class AAAAA state championship against Miller Grove, but nothing was done.

The position of the stanchions are supposed to be set so the baskets measure 15 feet from the foul line and the backboards sit 4 feet from the baseline.

"I went to the officials and told them, 'I don't care how long it takes to fix it, but we should get it right for our kids,'" Hood said.

Hood noticed there may be an issue while watching the Jonesboro boys play Thursday night in the Class AAAA championship game. At least five times, Hood said he watched a Jonesboro player rebound the ball and come down out of bounds. It also happened to Allatoona, and again to the McEachern girls early in the Class AAAAAA championship game against Tucker on Saturday. Both Pebblebrook and Westlake also had players come down with rebounds and step on the baseline.

Hood did not tell his players there was an issue before the game tipped off, but the extra length on the free throws made a difference to the Buccaneers. Hood said he had his players practice free throws last week with their eyes closed so they could shoot by feel and eliminate problems with depth perception.

Allatoona, which lost the game 50-48, shot 14-of-22 (63.6 percent) from the free-throw line.

Hood was adamant that the misplaced stanchions were not the reason they lost the game.

"I don't want it to sound like sour grapes," Hood said. "It was not the reason we lost the game. I just wanted to make sure it was fair for the kids—all the kids, not just ours."

Pebblebrook coach George Washington knew the goals were in the wrong place before his team took the floor for the Class AAAAAA boys championship game Saturday night. Washington said he asked the officials to fix them, but he was told no because it would take 1 and a half hours to fix.

The Falcons ended up losing the game to Westlake, 68-58, in overtime and the basket positions could have had an effect on the game.

"We're a jump shooting team and it affected us in the second half," he said, "but that's not why we lost."

Pebblebrook made only 3-of-14 shots from behind the arc and finished the game shooting at 38 percent. The Falcons actually shot free throws well. They made 11-of-12 in the first half before falling to 60 percent (6-of-10) in the second. Most of the other teams were not as lucky.

The 28 teams that played the three days of the tournament shot a combined 390-of-655 (59 percent) from the free-throw line—but success from beyond the arc was even harder to come by. The teams shot a combined 74-of-363 (20 percent) on 3-pointers.

Late Saturday night, the GHSA released a statement addressing the situation and saying there would be nothing done to alter the outcomes of any of the games.

"The goals were the same distance into the court at both ends of the floor," said GHSA Executive Director Gary Phillips. "The playing conditions were exactly the same for both teams on the court and for all of the 14 championship games that were played. So I can't see any reason we would consider changing the outcomes.

"Only one coach even mentioned a possible problem, and my basketball staff watched the games closely and did not notice any appreciable effect on the shooting or the play of any of the teams. Some of the teams even shot extremely well from both the floor and the free throw line. But, overall, it looked like typical championship play.

"While this certainly was not an ideal situation or one that we wanted to happen, we think the conditions were fair for all the teams. And, more importantly, it was the same for all the teams. We have plans to make sure this never happens again, but we have no plans to change anything that happened this week in Macon."

McEachern girls coach Phyllis Arthur, whose team played in the penultimate game of the weekend, said she knew the GHSA would not fix the problem.

"Yes, they should have changed it, but I knew they wouldn't," she said after her Lady Indians beat Tucker 71-51 to claim their third straight Class AAAAAA state title. "Because then the teams that played on that court the first two days, the ones that lost, could have used it as an excuse. This way everybody played on the same court."

The McEachern girls made 24-of-40 free throws and went 3-of-13 from behind the 3-point line.

Former Allatoona principal Scott Bursmith, who retired last year after a career that included 19 years as a high school basketball coach and five appearances in the state championship game, said there was no excuse for what happened.

"Somebody should lose their job," he said. "It means everyone was taking 16-foot free throws. The scene from 'Hoosiers' doesn't hold true. In Georgia, the baskets aren't the same distance they are everywhere else.

"I think everybody that played on the un-regulation court should share the state title."

GHSA SUFFERING FROM ITS OWN INEPTITUDE,
MARCH 13, 2016

The Georgia High School Association's PR nightmare continues.

The organization finally released a statement Friday apologizing for the improper setup of the goals on both ends of the floor in last week's state championship games at the Macon Coliseum.

"We offer our sincerest apologies to the players, coaches, and fans of all involved teams," executive director Gary Phillips said in the statement. "We consulted with the GHSA Board of Trustees and considered all options and alternatives. We concluded that the only reasonable resolution is to allow the games to stand as they were played and competed."

"We are conducting a thorough review of the current policies that should have prevented this and will be implementing new procedures to ensure that this never happens again."

While the GHSA might consider its apology sincere, it rings hollow with many of the coaches of the teams involved in the 14 championship games. Not just because it was a week late, but because of the way it was delivered. The coaches I spoke with said the statement was emailed to their respective athletic director, asking them to then pass it on to the coaches.

The GHSA couldn't take the time to email the coaches directly, let alone call them personally and apologize for possibly having a hand in ruining what was the team's biggest weekend of the season?

Last Saturday, in the middle of the final day of championship games, the GHSA admitted that the goals were set up "roughly 1 foot" further back than they should have been. It caused players at the free-throw line to shoot at a goal that was at least 16 feet away, rather than the standard 15 feet. It also meant that 3-pointers at the top of the key were a lot closer to the NBA distance of 23 feet, 9 inches at the top of the key, rather than the 19 feet, 9 inches for high school.

Friday's statement begs the question, does the GHSA think that, by releasing the apology, the case is closed? Based on a groundswell of emotion and the need for hard answers, it really looks like this is just the beginning. With the organization's complete lack of transparency, people are not going to let go of this anytime soon.

So far, according to coaches who had teams play last weekend, at least three formal protests have been filed. Donnie Griggers, the co-athletic director for Cobb County schools, said the district intends to file something of its own by mid-week. It would have come earlier, but the GHSA's statement likely forced some revisions.

Some coaches have said that state representatives are starting to get involved as well. On top of that, Eric Teusink, a corporate and real estate attorney from Atlanta, has started a petition at Change.org asking Gov. Nathan Deal and the Georgia General Assembly to reform the GHSA.

What Teusink and many of the coaches, school board members and state representatives want is additional oversight into how the GHSA makes its decisions and why. Considering the organization gets approximately 60 percent ($3 million) of its $5 million revenue (based on the GHSA financial report from the end of the 2014-15 school year) from member dues, fines and state tournament revenue, it has a point.

For the last week, I have made multiple calls and emails to Phillips asking for answers to some simple questions:

- Why, after Allatoona boys coach Markus Hood alerted officials to the problematic setup Friday night, was the court not fixed—not only then, but for the games on Saturday?
- The GHSA has said that steps will be taken to make sure mistakes like these never happen again. What are those steps?
- Does the GHSA continue to stand behind its statement that, because the court was set up the same way for both teams,

that it was fair to both teams—even those that are perimeter-based, jump-shooting teams?

- By playing the games, the GHSA broke its own constitution and bylaws by playing on a court that was not set up to standards set by the National Federation of High School Associations. How can they stand by those results?

Phillips has yet to respond.

Friday's statement said the GHSA consulted with its 10-person board of trustees, which includes Phillips as well as vice president Lisa Moore Williams—the former Osborne girls basketball coach now serving as principal of Mableton's Lindley Middle School—and Buford athletic director Dexter Wood—the former Lassiter, Marietta and Buford football coach.

With the trustees getting involved, they were contacted to help shed light on the situation. Questions to them included most of those asked to Phillips, but also:

- Why did it take a week to offer an apology?
- What were the options and alternatives considered before making the decision to let the results stand?

There was no response to emails sent to the majority of the board Friday, nor calls to Williams and Wood on Saturday.

Since this story broke last weekend, it has been the lead story on USA Today's high school sports web page, picked up by the Associated Press, Deadspin, Mashable and Forbes magazine, and it has run in newspapers from coast to coast. Right now, the GHSA is a national punching bag.

The longer the GHSA refuses to address the situation and offer some transparency, it's only going to get worse.

This story is nowhere near the end. In fact, it is likely just the beginning.

GHSA AVOIDING QUESTIONS ABOUT BASKETBALL TOURNAMENT DISCREPANCIES, APRIL 19, 2016

Georgia High School Association executive director Gary Phillips is great at making statements, but he's not very good at answering questions.

During his director's report Monday at the GHSA's spring executive committee meeting in Macon — just yards away from the Macon Coliseum arena where the stanchions were not set up properly for the state basketball championships last month — Phillips made another statement.

"At the point where we learned about the problem with the position of the basketball goals, we had 2 and a half games to play. We made the decision we were not to move the baskets. Everybody played at the same place," he said during the meeting, which was open to the public.

"What I can say is we are looking at our options. We're not going to talk about what those are. We'll make a statement when we decide what we are going to do and where we're going to do it. We feel like we've worked hard trying to explore what happened and we think we know, pretty much, some of the background information. By the time it was revealed to us and we found out we had a problem, we decided to finish where we were. That was our decision. With 2 and a half games left, we couldn't see what we could do with the other 11 and a half games.

"So, I just want to let you know, so you understand, it's not like we are ignoring this. We are working on this.

"We pride ourselves, if I can be allowed to say that, that we do a good job when we get to these state championship events. We regret what happened. We are going to go forward and do our best to make sure that never happens again."

There are a couple of concerns with this statement.

First, what are all the things the GHSA is looking into when it comes to figuring out what to do? It's been seven weeks since the tournament was played. Why can't Phillips stand up and just say, "From now on, we are going to make sure the stanchions are in the proper place by measuring to make sure the backboard is 4 feet from the baseline?"

More concerning is the adamant stance that the GHSA did not find out about the problem with the baskets until there were 2 and a half games left in the tournament.

One obvious problem is that Phillips has admitted that the GHSA knew at least prior to the two Class AAAAAA championship games that the baskets were wrong, and nothing was done to fix it.

But more importantly, Allatoona basketball coach Markus Hood has repeatedly said that he talked to the GHSA official overseeing his game prior to tipoff of the Class AAAAA championship game on Friday, the second of three consecutive days of championship games.

As it turns out, Hood is correct.

An email received by the MDJ through an open records request shows that John Ewalt, a member of the Greater Georgia Sports Officials Association and the lead on-court official in Allatoona's championship game, backs Hood's claim.

In the email dated March 14 and sent to GHSA basketball coordinator Ernie Yarbrough, Ewalt wrote:

"The Allatoona coach approached me near the scorer's table during the pregame warmups and stated that he felt the 'backboards were not lined up properly.' I asked him what he meant and he stated, 'They are too close to the end line.'"

Ewalt, in his email, then said he attempted to search out for Earl

Etheridge, the GHSA's on-site representative for the basketball tournament.

"After this conversation I initially looked for Mr. Etheridge because he had just conducted the pregame meeting with the coaches and officials, but did not locate him. So, I spoke to the person at midcourt who was acting as the floor manager (dressed in a GHSA shirt and GHSA Event Staff credential) and distributing the balls. The Allatoona coach then proceeded to present his concern and the GHSA representative stated, 'the backboards are the same on both ends of the floor, so let's play ball.'"

When Phillips was asked about the discrepancy, he refused to explain.

"I'm not going to speak to that," he told the MDJ on Monday. "I'm not going to speak to that. I know what that email says, but I'm not going to respond."

Phillips also said he had no idea who the floor manager of the Class AAAAA championship game was, but he said that person's job was to help the tournament director run the tournament.

The fact that the GHSA representative, determined worthy of helping the tournament director run the tournament, doesn't have the basketball knowledge—or at least the wherewithal—to get their boss when a coach brings a potential serious issue to their attention says a lot more about the GHSA than Phillips' statements.

Either way, the GHSA knew on Friday night, with seven games—or half the tournament to play—the baskets were set up wrong and did nothing to fix it. The fact that that was not communicated to Phillips and/or Yarbrough until late Saturday is no excuse.

At this point, there is nothing the GHSA can do—or will—do to change the results of the tournament. The coaches knew that wasn't going to happen from the outset. All they want is the GHSA to be transparent about the situation.

Phillips said he has been advised "not to speak to the media about this." He said he's made a definitive statement and added, "Until we have something more positive to announce, I'm not going to have anything to say."

Based on this, Phillips isn't going to be talking for a long time.

GHSA MOVING BASKETBALL CHAMPIONSHIPS OUT OF MACON, MAY 20, 2016

After nearly a half-century of holding at least a portion of its state basketball finals at the Macon Coliseum, the Georgia High School Association is taking the tournaments on the road.

The 2017 state finals are going to be played in two locations next year. The University of Georgia's Stegeman Coliseum will host two days of games on March 8 and 9, while Georgia Tech's McCamish Pavilion will be the likely host of games on March 10 and 11.

The information was obtained by the MDJ through an open records request.

A joint announcement between the colleges and the GHSA is expected to be made around Memorial Day or in early June.

When reached by email for additional comment, GHSA executive director Gary Phillips released a statement.

"Any change of venue is not finalized," he said. "Therefore we are not prepared to comment at this time. Any statement would be premature."

Phone messages and emails requesting additional comment from Georgia and Georgia Tech officials were not returned.

The move is in part because of a mishap at the Macon Coliseum during the state championship games March 3-5, when the basketball stanchions were not anchored in the proper positions. That left teams to play on a court not set up to standards of the National Federation of State High School Associations.

The problem was brought to the attention of the GHSA at the halfway point of the tournament on March 4 by Allatoona boys basketball coach Markus Hood, prior to the Buccaneers' Class AAAAA title game against Miller Grove. The GHSA released a statement March 5, saying the organization was not made aware of the problem until there were 2 and a half games remaining on the schedule, and at that point, the problem would not be fixed.

There were also issues with restroom and locker facilities at the Macon Coliseum, along with concessions and parking, in which teams were charged $20 to park their school bus.

GHSA associate director Ernie Yarborough, in an email dated March 17, reached out to officials at the Infinite Energy Center in Duluth, inquiring about potential open dates. The 12,750-seat arena has hosted the basketball finals before.

"I know during our last communication you stated that 2019 would be the first possibility to play the GHSA basketball championships in the arena, but in light of some of the recent problems we have encountered in Macon we are being compelled to secure another venue moving forward," Yarborough wrote.

Moving the tournament from the Macon Coliseum would be a first. The arena opened in 1968 and has hosted at least some of the state basketball tournament games every year.

A person familiar with the situation said the GHSA has not yet contacted officials at the Macon Centreplex about the pending move.

Once the tournament was completed on March 5, the GHSA wasted little time in reaching out to prospective host sites.

The first contact with the University of Georgia was in an email dated March 12, with a follow-up by Yarborough directed to John Bateman, the university's assistant athletic director for marketing. That email said the GHSA had tried unsuccessfully to secure Stegeman Coliseum for state championship games for 15 years.

Last week, everything seemed to have come together.

An email dated May 10 from Bateman confirmed the university's involvement.

"Just spoke with Gary Phillips and told him we were prepared to take the next steps with plans to host GHSA boys and girls basketball state championships March 8-9, 2017. Like us, he's excited about hosting games in Stegeman."

Later in that same email, Bateman, in a summary of the call with Phillips, referenced that Georgia Tech is "moving forward with plans to host."

An email also dated May 10 from David Grice, the associate athletic director for facilities, operations and events at Georgia Tech, confirmed Bateman's statement.

"We have confirmed that the facility is available for March 10 & 11," Grice said. "The next piece of the puzzle is a discussion with parking services… Once we have that discussion, my hope is that we can finalize an agreement. We are excited about the potential to host GHSA basketball at McCamish Pavilion."

Pebblebrook boys basketball coach George Washington, whose team lost the Class AAAAAA state championship game to Westlake, said a move to the college campuses would be great news.

"That is awesome," Washington said. "I would love to play at either one of those venues."

DIXON LEAVES GEORGIA TECH, AND KSU FAITHFUL, BUZZING, NOVEMBER 16, 2010

For KSU fans, enjoy the memory of Monday night.

Final score, Kennesaw State 80, Georgia Tech 63.

The win was special. The win was historic.

If you are an Owls' fan on campus today, give an extra special shout out to Spencer Dixon. The KSU sophomore point guard, who played his high school basketball in the shadows of the KSU Convocation Center at Kennesaw Mountain, was the best player on the floor.

He was a step faster than the fastest Yellow Jacket, and he was waiting for this moment. Unlike many players that live for their chance to shine, the moment wasn't too big for Dixon.

"I asked Spencer to quarterback this team and lead it to victory," Kennesaw State coach Tony Ingle said. "I asked him, 'Can you do that?' and he said, 'Yes.'"

Boy did he mean it.

After picking up what he called two "silly" fouls early, he came back in the game with 10:52 left before halftime. Ingle said the decision to put him back in was a gamble, because a third foul would have left him on the bench likely watching Georgia Tech eliminate KSU's early lead.

"It was a big gamble," Ingle said. "But he's got five fouls and we had to have him. There was no way we were going to win the ball game without Spencer (on the floor)."

This morning, Ingle and Dixon are splitting the jackpot.

When Dixon reentered the game, KSU held an 18-11 lead. Six minutes later, after a Dixon layup, the Owls were up 36-16 and on their way to a 41-26 lead at the break. During the run, he scored only four points and had two assists, but it was his ability to control the game that kept the Owls in front.

In the second half, he proved to be the difference in the game, and he did it suffering from leg cramps.

"We wanted to play more people but we knew we couldn't," Ingle said. "We had to keep the guys in the game. We knew their teammates would pump them up, but I had to call timeouts to let (him) rest. During the timeouts, Spencer was lying on the floor working out his cramps. Then, Markeith said he was cramping up and then I started getting stomach cramps thinking about playing without these guys."

Cramps aside, Georgia Tech kept making runs in the second half, and each time, Dixon found a way to answer. The Yellow Jackets went on a 9-1 run to pull within 49-43 with 13:37 to play. A Dixon 3 got the record, sellout crowd of 4,784 back in the game. After another 6-2 run to pull within five, Dixon let a 3-pointer from the top of the key fly.

"He just stepped back and launched it," Yellow Jackets' coach Paul Hewitt said. "You almost knew it was going in. You could tell he was feeling it."

Dixon knew he was feeling it, too.

When the ball went up he held the pose and took two steps back. It was just enough time for the ball to slide gently through the net leading to the biggest smile of the night.

"I knew it was in," Dixon said. "There was no doubt."

He finished off the Jackets in style. Dixon scored 27 points, 18 in the second half, with six assists. The last of the assists came after stealing the ball from former high school nemesis, Walton's Glen Rice, Jr. The steal turned into a perfect lead pass to Markeith Cummings which turned into a rim-rattling, crowd pleasing, building shaking dunk.

As the final seconds clicked off the clock, Dixon ran around like a little kid opening presents at Christmas. His smile said it all as he pumped up the crowd, and when the buzzer sounded KSU had the biggest win in school history.

"It's an all-time high (for us,)" he said. "For a team from the A-Sun to take down Georgia Tech it means a lot."

Before the game, Ingle told his team he wanted their dream game Monday night. By the time it was over, all Dixon wanted were a few sweet dreams thinking about more 3s with some zzzzz.

"I'm tired," he said. "I'm going home and going to sleep."

Hopefully he slept well, because for one night, Monday night, when Kennesaw State beat Georgia Tech 80-63, Dixon was one of the best players in college basketball.

BERENATO HEEDS THE CALL TO COME TO KSU,
APRIL 16, 2016

Cindy Gillam knew she could not stop talking.

She was on the phone with Agnus Berenato, and Gillam knew, if she even allowed herself a pause to take a long breath, she may lose the chance to bring the former Georgia Tech and Pittsburgh women's basketball coach to Kennesaw State.

The conversation lauding the opportunities at KSU lasted almost two hours, not ending until Berenato pulled her car into Key Largo, Florida.

"She went on and on and on," Berenato said. "All I wanted to tell her I had a J-O-B. I had a job and I'm not going back into coaching."

Gillam, a former four-year starter under Berenato's sister, Bernadette McGlade, at Georgia Tech and now an executive assistant in the office of the associate vice president of enrollment services at KSU, convinced Berenato to sleep on the idea and left her with one last thought.

"I told her, 'If your butt is not on the court, you're wasting the gifts God gave you,'" Gillam said.

Then, she got a somewhat unexpected answer.

"You sound like (my sister)," Gillam said Berenato told her. "She told me I needed to get back on the court."

By the time they talked the next day, KSU had a coaching candidate.

"Did you know Kennesaw State had over 100 majors and 33,000 students?" Gillam said Berenato asked her.

Moments later, for all intents and purposes, the Owls had a head coach.

"Darn you, Cindy Gillam," Gillam remembered Berenato saying. "I didn't sleep last night. I've got chills. I can't believe I'm considering it."

On Thursday, Berenato was introduced as the seventh women's basketball coach in Kennesaw State history. She brings a 444-413 career record and 11 postseason appearances in 29 seasons, and at 6-foot-1, she could be an intimidating figure if she wanted to be.

Instead, the winningest coach in Pittsburgh history and second-winningest at Georgia Tech is high-energy, no-nonsense and doesn't seem to be politically correct.

She has a boisterous sense of humor and can tell a proper story.

She yells, screams, motivates and hip-checks unsuspecting reporters.

She sweet-talks people into large fundraising donations, high-fives athletic directors, appears to know when to kick her team in the backside and hugs everyone in sight.

Based on first impressions, Berenato has never met a stranger, which is why she already refers to her new team as part of her family.

"We all have mentors in our lives to drive us to get better," Berenato said. "To my new ladies, I am so excited and overwhelmed at the opportunity to teach, to coach, to mentor and to love you. I think, together, we will learn and explore opportunities to excel. We will represent Kennesaw State University."

More than anything, Berenato comes across as a leader, and that's why Gillam zeroed in on her and didn't let go.

"I'm passionate about basketball," Gillam said, "and I want the women's basketball program to get to the level it's supposed to be. When I was asked to be on the search committee, the only person I could think of was Coach B."

Berenato has a lot of work to do.

Kennesaw State had only one winning season in the last seven years.

Since joining the Atlantic Sun in the 2005-06 season, the Owls have never finished higher than fourth in conference play. Even more disturbing is, considering the success of the high school basketball teams in Cobb and Cherokee counties, there have been a combined five players from the two-county area over the same time period.

Berenato has been out of coaching for the last three years, doing a lot of television work and motivational speaking. Now, she gets to see if she can motivate her new team to the top of the A-Sun.

Thursday was a good start.

"We are going to get rings," she said. "We are going to get rings. Yes, we are going to cut the nets down."

She also gave a shout-out to her friend, Gillam.

"Thirty-five years ago, she was a student-athlete at Georgia Tech," Berenato said. "I was a coach at Rider. I was young, energetic, crazy and I berated officials. She liked that and never forgot it. Well, Cindy, I'm no longer young. I'm still crazy, but I no longer berate officials. It doesn't do any good.

"Your perseverance is the only reason I'm standing here."

It's too early to tell if Gillam deserves any kind of a finder's fee, since Berenato has yet to step on the floor at the KSU Convocation Center, but for the first time in a long time, the women's basketball program feels like it has life — or at least someone that's larger than life.

Hopefully, Berenato can pay off that finder's fee in wins.

GEORGIA'S BUCKLIN KNOWS ALL ABOUT FINAL FOUR, MARCH 17, 2011

Now that the anticipation on whether or not Georgia would make the NCAA tournament field has passed, it's time to turn to Matt Bucklin to find out what it's like to make it to the Final Four.

Bucklin, a former Pope standout who served as a backup guard for the Bulldogs, is the nephew of Michigan State coach Tom Izzo. He can draw on his uncle's experience of reaching six Final Fours since 1995, including the last two.

Bucklin talks basketball with his uncle often, and he will be able to tell his Georgia teammates what it is like to be on the doorstep of a national championship after attending several Final Fours to cheer for Izzo's Spartans.

As No. 10-seed Georgia prepares to play No. 7 Washington in Friday night's late game in Charlotte, N.C., Bucklin can tell his teammates about the sounds, sights and smells associated with college basketball's biggest event. He can talk about the electricity in the building at game time and about the former players who come to root for their former teams.

"When I became a member of the (Bulldogs), I had to fill out forms for the media guide," Bucklin said. "One of the questions it asked is, 'Who is the most famous person you've met?" and I answered Magic Johnson. They came back to me and asked where I met Magic Johnson, and I told them I sat and talked basketball with him at the Final Four."

Of course, all Bucklin's previous experiences have been by himself.

Now, he has the opportunity to enhance that experience as part of a team. That's something that seemed unlikely when he followed in his brother Mike's footsteps. After the elder Bucklin played as a walk-on at Georgia from 2002-04, Matt did the same when he tried out for the Bulldogs in the summer of 2008.

In Bucklin's freshman year, Georgia went 12-20 under then-coach Dennis Felton. Then his sophomore year started with a new coach in Mark Fox, but the record didn't get much better. The Bulldogs finished 2009-10 at 14-17.

But something changed heading into this season.

Fox put together a nucleus of a team that could win. And the coach was so impressed with the way Bucklin approached the game that the 6-foot, 170-pound former Greyhound was put on scholarship.

"He earned it," Fox said. "He's done everything we have asked him to do. Matt works hard and has a high basketball IQ. If we need him to play, he can come in and play anywhere on the floor, from the 1 to the 4."

In doing the hard work, Bucklin has earned the never-ending respect of the scholarship players who were there before him.

"I'm really happy for him," said teammate and fellow Cobb product Dustin Ware, formerly of North Cobb Christian. "He earned it, because Matt usually had to work harder than everyone else and he couldn't afford to mess up. Because if he did, not being on scholarship, he would have been easily expendable."

Bucklin's career numbers likely won't get him into the Georgia record books—in three seasons, he's played a total of 26 minutes—but that hasn't kept him from becoming a crowd favorite.

During blowouts at Stegeman Coliseum, it doesn't take long for the student section to start chanting, "We want Bucklin." He rewarded his fan base with the first basket of his college career in Georgia's home finale against LSU.

Bucklin connected on a hanging jumper at the free-throw line with 25 seconds left in the game. Not only did he make the basket, but he was fouled, leading to a three-point play that brought his career point total to four.

The basket put Georgia up 20 and helped the Bulldogs earn their 20th win of the season.

Now it's on to the NCAA tournament.

Unless Friday's game is another blowout, Bucklin likely won't get off the bench. But like he's done his entire career, he'll watch, listen and be ready if Fox needs him.

It's those qualities, Fox said, that would make Bucklin a good basketball coach one day.

Maybe Bucklin will follow his uncle into the family business one day. But right now, he would rather face Izzo in the NCAA tournament. To do that, Georgia and Michigan State would both have to reach the championship game in Houston, something that would likely be just fine for both.

And it would make for a good conversation at the next family reunion.

FOR GREG MATTA, OHIO STATE COACH IS SIMPLY LITTLE BROTHER, MARCH 30, 2012

As the final minutes of the Ohio State-Syracuse game ran off the clock last Saturday, Greg Matta's phone started ringing.

He started hearing from friends and family members that he either hadn't talked to in decades, or, in some cases, had never heard of.

Not one of them wanted to talk about old times or how Matta was doing, and nobody was trying to congratulate him for his North Cobb Christian basketball team going 28-1 this past season. They all wanted to talk about his brother—Thad Matta, the head coach of the Ohio State Buckeyes—and whether Greg thought Thad could get them tickets to the Final Four in New Orleans.

"Can Thad get (them) tickets? Thad can't get me tickets," joked Greg, who's 2 and a half years older.

He said a few callers at least made small talk first, but they eventually all got around to asking the same question. And, when Matta relayed the bad news, many then changed the subject.

"What about shirts and hats?"

"People just don't understand that side of the business," Matta said. "Coaches don't have time for that stuff, and with Thad, he's just focused on one thing—Kansas."

Ohio State will play the Jayhawks in the late game Saturday night, about 30 minutes after the Louisville-Kentucky showdown opens up the Final Four at the Superdome.

Matta will be one of the lucky ones in attendance, thanks to the folks in the Ohio State traveling party. But, before anyone thinks Matta was getting a freebie, he made it very clear he was paying for his own tickets.

For Matta, Saturday's game—and, hopefully, the championship two days later—is a glimpse inside his brother's world, and that's college basketball at the highest level. And when Greg sees the pressure Thad is under, it makes him appreciate his job at North Cobb Christian even more.

Matta tried the college route before. Twice, he was a member of Tony Ingle's staff at Kennesaw State, and he was a rumored candidate for the Owls' job when it came open following the 2010-11 season.

Right now, however, Matta says he is content with helping young players on his own team like Stephon Jelks and Hunter Ware reach their potential.

"I love working at the high school level," Matta said. "Yes, you always dream about that big-time college job and going to the Final Four, but I like sleeping in my own bed."

Just not this weekend.

Matta said he planned to leave for the Big Easy today, and while he may not be coaching on the collegiate level, he knows plenty about the four schools that will take the court at the Superdome.

Matta said he likes Kentucky in the first game. He expects the Wildcats to run, and he said the key will be the big guys—All-American Anthony Davis, Terrance Jones and Michael Kidd-Gilchrist—getting all the way to the basket when they are in transition.

For Louisville, the only way the Cardinals can win is by slowing the pace and getting Kentucky to play a half-court game.

In Game 2, he likes the Buckeyes — naturally — to take care of Kansas. This time, Ohio State will be at full-strength because All-American Jared Sullinger did not play against the Jayhawks when Kansas beat the Buckeyes early in the season.

"I like Ohio State. (Aaron) Craft can get all the guys where they need to be. Sullinger has to stay out of foul trouble, and if (Deshaun) Thomas can stay humble and crash the boards, they should win."

As for a potential championship game between Kentucky and Ohio State — does the question really need to be asked?

"Ohio State all the way."

This is actually the second time Matta will see his brother coach in the Final Four. The first time was 2007, when Ohio State lost to Florida at the Georgia Dome.

The following season, Matta took North Cobb Christian to a perfect season, which included winning the National Association of Christian Athletes Division I national championship.

So, it begs the question — has Thad called Greg for any advice on how to win a national championship?

"Thad doesn't ask my advice, because he's afraid that I might give it to him."

BREAST CANCER PRESENTS AGNUS BERENATO
WITH HER TOUGHEST FOE YET,
NOVEMBER 24, 2018

KENNESAW—Agnus Berenato is a lot like many of us.

She's busy.

As the women's basketball coach at Kennesaw State, she has practices, recruiting visits, meetings, games and a hundred other things on her plate at any one time.

For her, putting off a doctor's appointment because of her schedule isn't an uncommon practice—with one exception. She always goes for her scheduled mammograms, and the one she had earlier this summer likely saved her life.

"My mom died of breast cancer," Berenato said recently. "My sister (Mary) had breast cancer, and my brother died of cancer. I don't miss my mammograms."

Berenato always had traditional mammograms, but this time she listened to her sister. In a not so subtle way, Mary implored Berenato to get a 3D mammogram—something she had never heard of.

According to the Mayo Clinic, a traditional two-dimensional mammogram only gets about four images from the top and the side of the breast. A three-dimensional mammogram allows doctors to be more accurate in the detection and diagnosis of cancer. It provides nearly 300 images and allows the radiologist to see breast tissue in greater detail.

Following the procedure and follow-up ultrasounds, the 61-year-old Berenato was diagnosed with Stage 1 breast cancer. It meant the disease was caught early, and the cancer cells were contained to a single area.

She said the diagnosis did not faze her. Having dealt with the disease in the family before, she knew she wanted to handle it head-on with an aggressive schedule—surgery, radiation and chemotherapy.

Berenato underwent surgery in September and, when she went in for a follow-up appointment, the detail-oriented coach in her took over.

She had her radiation schedule all mapped out—five days a week for 6 and a half weeks. She knew what day she wanted to start, when the treatments would end and how many basketball games she may need to miss.

However, Berenato's plan didn't go the way she wanted.

"When they told me they found more cancer and I needed a second surgery, you could have knocked me over with a feather," Berenato said.

That was only half of the issue.

"The worst part of the whole thing was the genetic testing," she said.

Berenato had to be tested to find out if she could have passed on a gene that would have given her three daughters and two sons an approximately 50-percent chance of contracting breast cancer.

"When I got the phone call, I broke down and cried," Berenato said. "It was negative. It took me 30 minutes to control myself so I could let my family know. It was as if the weight of the world was taken off my shoulders."

In October, Berenato underwent the second surgery, which eliminated the remainder of the cancer. She said the players and coaches were at her house the following day after each surgery, preparing meals and making sure she had what she needed.

Berenato will likely begin radiation treatments in December, but, as the true teacher she is, she gave her 13 players and four-member coaching staff an education on the disease.

"I promised to educate them so they don't have to be afraid of cancer," she said.

Berenato started the class by hitting the players with some eye-opening details based on the information she had been given by her doctors.

"Four of you are going to get this disease," Berenato told them.

She said the best way for them to understand was to show them exactly what had taken place, so Berenato bared all. She showed the scars, including the points of entry where the doctors went in, and she explained what they did.

Berenato said this started a dialogue and brought many questions, but she feels like not only do the players and coaches have a better understanding of what is going on with her, but it has brought the group closer in their day-to-day relationships.

For the most part, the diagnosis, surgery, treatment and fight have not kept Berenato from doing what she loves best—coaching basketball—although she has had to throttle down the accelerator a little bit.

The team recently took a trip to New Jersey to play in the Seton Hall Tip-Off tournament. Instead of accompanying her team to dinner or movies, Berenato instead spent that time at the hotel sleeping and getting the extra rest she needs.

"I've never been so tired in my whole life," Berenato said, "and I'm one of those people, the first thing when I wake up is say, 'When can I go to bed?'

"It's a different fatigue. I don't know what it is, because I'm not sick."

Throughout the ordeal, Berenato said her staff of associate head coach Khadija Head, assistants Sherill Baker and Lanay Montgomery and director of basketball operations Chelby Coley has been outstanding.

"I'm totally confident in them," Berenato said. "They could take (over for) the whole season if necessary."

For Berenato, it is nice to know her staff and players have her back. For the staff and players, Berenato couldn't prove she had their back in a bigger, or better, way. She also hopes that by talking with them and by letting everyone know about what happened, it can help other people along the way.

"It was huge catching this early at Stage 1. Had I not gotten this mammogram …," Berenato said, tailing off and wondering what could have happened.

"Why wouldn't you go and get it done so you can get the report that, 'Yep, you're good,' or, 'We have an issue.' It's a little blip if you find it and get it done quickly, but, if left unattended, that blip can cost you your life."

HARPER, SEXTON STILL MAKING PEBBLEBROOK PROUD, APRIL 3, 2019

When you have two potential superstars on your team, sometimes it's hard to get them to share the ball.

Pebblebrook boys basketball coach George Washington said that was not an issue with Jared Harper and Collin Sexton.

"I would give them goals each game, but I eventually had to stop that." Washington said. "One game, I told them they each needed to get 10 assists in a game. They came down the court on a fast break and they kept passing it back-and-forth. Neither wanted to score because they were trying to get the assist."

Harper and Sexton played together only one season in 2015-16, after Sexton transferred from Hillgrove. They helped lead Pebblebrook to the state title game, where the Falcons lost to Westlake 68-58 in overtime.

Harper helped lead Pebblebrook to the title game the previous year, while Sexton led the Falcons to the quarterfinals the year following. Washington said the impact the two players had on the program could not accurately be measured, and to see the way the pair have represented their alma mater makes their former coach proud.

"My chest is puffing out a little bit," Washington said.

Over the last few years, Washington has put a lot of good players into the Division I college ranks, including Dwight Murray (Incarnate

Word), Mervin James (Canisius), Ty Hudson (Clemson/Jacksonville State) and Derek Ogbeide (Georgia). It has allowed Pebblebrook to become a national brand, and that brand is going to get some extra television time Saturday when Harper leads Auburn onto the floor of the Final Four against Virginia in Minneapolis.

Harper stole the show last Sunday when he helped Auburn beat Kentucky in overtime, scoring 12 of his team-high 26 points in the extra session. It was a performance, Washington said, that showed the maturity and development of Harper's game, now that he is in his junior year of college.

"He's setting up teammates to let them get open shots," Washington said. "When they need him to score, he goes and gets baskets. Not a lot has changed since high school. He's been a great leader, and he's not afraid to tell his teammates what they need to hear. I think he's gotten better with the delivery of the message, but, sometimes, you have to be rough around the edges."

Harper enters Saturday's game averaging 17.5 points and 6.5 assists per game in the tournament, which included wins over blue-blood programs Kansas, North Carolina and Kentucky over the last three rounds. Those averages are slightly higher than Harper's season averages of 15.4 points and 5.8 assists, for which he was named to the All-Southeastern Conference second team for the second straight year.

"He's willing to do whatever it takes to win," Washington said.

The same can be said for Sexton, but instead of getting another chance at one shining moment at Alabama, he left for the NBA after his freshman year.

As the No. 8 overall draft pick, Sexton landed on one of the worst teams in the league—the now LeBron James-less Cleveland Cavaliers—but just like Harper, Sexton has been playing his best basketball as the season comes to a close.

He is averaging 16.6 points per game and has dished out 222 assists.

Those numbers are both third for rookies behind only Dallas' Luka Doncic and Atlanta's Trae Young. But over the last 21 games, Sexton is averaging 21 points a night. Over the last 13, that number is 24 points a game.

Sexton was passed over for playing in the Rising Stars Challenge, a game between the best rookies and second-year players during the NBA's annual All-Star weekend. He took that snub as a challenge and now has worked himself into a likely spot on the NBA's All-Rookie Team.

Sexton did it through hard work.

After practices, Sexton stays in the gym and shoots an extra 300 to 500 jump shots. Sometimes, he comes back and shoots 100 to 200 jumpers after a game.

Sexton is now shooting 41.4 percent from the 3-point line, helping him put together a streak of seven consecutive games in which he scored 23 points or more, becoming the first rookie to reach that mark since Tim Duncan in 1998.

"He's playing really well," Washington said. "This is what happens when the game slows down. The same for Jared. Now, they are able to read things two, three, four plays ahead."

For Washington, getting to watch the development of Harper and Sexton has been a treat. Almost any night of the week, he's been able to turn on the TV and see the foundation he helped build at Pebblebrook.

However, the on-the-court success is only a small part of what makes Washington smile.

"They have represented (Pebblebrook) and the program so well," he said. "They have never done anything wrong. They've never gotten into any trouble."

Washington also said whenever Harper and Sexton are on a break, they come back to Mableton and work out in their old gym. They also help the current group of Falcons when they can.

But the best part is when they call their old coach to check in.

Washington said he recently talked to Harper during Auburn's NCAA Tournament run and was told the best thing he could hear.

"'I always have time for your call, coach,'" Washington said Harper told him.

The second-best thing he could have heard was what Harper told him next.

"'Coach, I have tickets for you.'"

Washington will head up to Minnesota this weekend to watch his former point guard potentially lead Auburn into Monday's national championship game against either Texas Tech or Michigan State.

Meanwhile, with the Cavs still having a good chance at landing the first pick in June's NBA draft, they could have a starting lineup that includes Sexton, Kevin Love and their selection of Murray State star Ja Morant or Duke phenoms Zion Williamson and RJ Barrett.

With that, Washington may be heading to Cleveland as early as next season to watch Sexton make his playoff debut.

By that time, Harper may be in the league, too. It would just be another superlative for Pebblebrook basketball.

"I'm very proud," Washington said.

He should be.

ONCE A WARRIOR, ALWAYS A WARRIOR: HALL INDUCTEE INGLE LOOKS BACK ON CHEROKEE'S RUN TO TITLE GAME, APRIL 24, 2009

KENNESAW—Kennesaw State men's basketball coach Tony Ingle remembers the first time he walked into Cherokee High School as he interviewed to be the coach of the Warriors' boys basketball team.

The year was 1978 and, up to that point, the Cherokee girls team had won six state titles, including a title in 1976. With a strong basketball tradition in place, Ingle said he was excited and ready to learn about the history of the boys program.

"On one side, leading to the gym, there were pictures and trophies of all the girls had won," Ingle said. "When I went over to the other side to see what the boys had done, I found one sign. It said, 'No food or drinks in the gym.'"

The situation may have had other coaches running for the door. Ingle decided it was an opportunity he couldn't pass up.

"We embraced the girls' team success," he said. "I figured if they could do it, we can do it. So, we rolled up our sleeves and went to work."

Four years later, Ingle had the Warriors playing for a state title and, to this day, he is the only boys basketball coach to have done so at the school.

For this reason, and all the success he helped build at Cherokee during his seven years as coach, Ingle will be inducted into the Cherokee County Sports Hall of Fame tonight at First Baptist Church of Canton.

Ingle will join the other 2009 inductees—Danny Cronic, John Milford and brothers Benny and Bobby Fitzgerald—to bring the number of hall members to 71.

"I'm flattered," he said. "It's an honor I can't really put into words. It's a special time for me and my family."

Ingle also said his days as the Warriors' coach helped him develop his coaching philosophy.

"It was there I learned about the awesome responsibility a coach has," he said. "As a coach, you have to have enthusiasm. You have to be up and you have to look for the good in each situation."

When he started at Cherokee, Ingle started rebuilding the program by getting people to talk about it. Twice, in games against Marietta, he used unorthodox approaches that teams are not likely to recreate today.

"One game, he had his guys doing cartwheels down the court," said

Charlie Hood, who recently retired after a 37-year tenure as Marietta's head coach.

"And then there was that game where they used the dead cockroach play."

The Blue Devils came into the game ranked among the state's top and had future NBA sharpshooter Dale Ellis leading the team. During the game, Ingle told three of his players to fall to the floor and flop around, almost as if they were having convulsions.

"If you are an opponent and someone does that, what are you going to do?" Ingle said. "Dale stopped, was concerned and tried to help him."

Meanwhile, the Warriors threw the ball down court to John Thomas for a layup.

Building around Thomas and his brother, Robert, it wasn't long before Cherokee didn't need gimmicks to get noticed anymore.

Then came the 1981-82 season.

After a successful regular season, the Warriors started a playoff run which made them look like a team of destiny. They opened the post-season with a 63-61 win over Decatur's Shamrock High before beating Morrow, 45-38, to advance to the final four.

Cherokee won the semifinal game, 52-50, over Laney only to see the title run fall one win short when the Warriors dropped a 68-67 decision to Campbell in the Class AAAA championship game.

Ingle left Cherokee after the 1985 season to follow his ultimate dream of being a college coach.

"I had to," he said. "I knew I couldn't win a national championship in high school.

Ingle started at Gordon College, a junior college in Barnesville. From there he coached at Alabama-Huntsville, BYU and was a scout for the Utah Jazz before coming back to the area to take the reins of Kennesaw State's men's basketball program in 1999.

Ingle led the Owls to the pinnacle of Division II, winning a national title in 2004.

Now, as Ingle tries to recreate that success at the Division I level, and no matter how well the Owls do, Ingle will always have fond memories of his time at Cherokee.

"It was an honor (to coach there)," he said. "I appreciate this honor, but what means more to me is all the players I had the privilege to have as members of our team."

GOLF

A MARIETTAN SCORES THE MASTERS: FARRAR WILL TAKE A SEAT FOR GOLF HISTORY NEXT FOUR DAYS, APRIL 5, 2007

The names roll off the tongue like a who's-who in the world of golf — Nicklaus, Palmer, Player, Watson, Mickelson and Woods. The game's greats, as they do every year, have arrived in Augusta for the Masters.

Many of those players will tee off today, starting the 71st annual competition for the Green Jacket and first major of the year and, as they make their tour of Augusta National Golf Club, they will have to pass another long time fixture of the tournament, Marietta native Ken Farrar.

Farrar is working his 31st Masters Tournament as a volunteer stationary scorer this week, and as he has for the previous 15 years, he will be spending his day watching the world's best golfers play the 13th hole, the picturesque par-5 last leg of Amen Corner.

"I get to see all the golf I want to see," said Farrar, a 52-year old orthodontist who carries a 4-handicap at Marietta Country Club, "and I've seen some other interesting things."

He said he got to see Tiger Woods putt from the back of the two-tiered green down to a front hole location and then into a tributary of the fabled Rae's Creek when the world's No. 1 player showed that even he is human.

"If you know anything about the Masters, you know the greens are lightning fast, probably running about a 15 on the stimpmeter," Farrar said. "When Tiger hit his putt it was barely moving as it went over the hill but then it picked up speed and rolled right off the green and into the water."

He also saw something that has happened only three times before in the history of the tournament. In 1994, Farrar was at his post when Jeff Maggert holed a 3-iron from 222 yards out to join Gene Sarazen (1935) and Bruce Devlin (1967) as the only players to make a double-eagle in the Masters.

"This was before we fed all the scores into a palm pilot," Farrar said, whose job as a stationary scorer is to count the number of strokes each player makes as they play the hole. He reports it to central control, which relays the information to workers at manual scoreboards around the course. "So I had to get on the radio and call central and say, 'Jeff Maggert, No. 13, two.' The next thing I hear is, 'did you say two? A double-eagle?' I went around with them for about 10 minutes before they would believe me."

Of course, if there is a drawback to being a stationary scorer at Augusta National during the Masters, is just that, being stationary. Unlike the patrons who can come and go, Farrar has to remain in one spot, on some days that means it could be 12 hours or more, but that doesn't mean he doesn't know what is going on. More often than not, he can tell who is doing what by the roar of the crowd.

"You can tell the difference between an eagle roar and a birdie roar," Farrar said. "And you can tell when Arnold Palmer rolls in a 30-foot putt for par. It's something completely different."

Palmer provided Farrar with his most emotional memory in 2004 when "The King" played in his 50th and final Masters.

"Everyone knew it was his final round and he got a standing ovation everywhere he went," Farrar said. "When he came around to 13 and the crowd cheered in appreciation all I could do was cry."

However, in all the time he spent at 13, no one could prepare him for the strangest request he has ever received.

"I was out there a couple hours before the players started to come through when a man carrying a small box came up and said, 'My father's wishes were to have his ashes spread in Rae's Creek. Would it be OK if I do that here?' I just looked at my coworker and shrugged my shoulders and we let him. I didn't have the heart to tell him it wasn't Rae's Creek he was putting his father in, it's a tributary that leads to it, so I figured Dad would reach Rae's Creek soon enough."

Farrar began playing the game of golf at age 12, but his first recollection of The Masters was less than exciting.

"I was at the home we were staying at," Farrar said. "When my parents came back they told me about the tournament. At the time I didn't think much of it."

That changed when the University of Georgia graduate entered dental school at the Medical College of Georgia in Augusta. As a 22-year old golf addict, Farrar was surprised to find out the same person, Sherman Lester, who's home he stayed at eight years before, was in charge of finding the scorers for the tournament. When Lester asked if Farrar wanted a job, it didn't take long to think about it.

"It took me about nine nanoseconds to say yes," Farrar said.

Since then he has been present for a lot of golf history. Farrar remembers the joy and loud roars when a 46-year-old Jack Nicklaus won a sixth Masters title in 1986. He recalls Greg Norman's too-painful-to-watch back nine collapse in 1996 when he turned a 6-shot lead after three rounds into a 5-stroke loss to Nick Faldo after shooting a final round 78. He was also there when Woods told everyone he was here to stay with a record-setting 12-shot win in 1997. But as much fun as he has had as a scorer, his friends, family and acquaintances are mostly jealous of what he gets to do after the tournament.

The biggest benefit of being a volunteer comes during the last week the course is open in May before it shuts down for the hot summer months. That week is when the tournament workers and volunteers have the opportunity to play Augusta National, something the majority of golf fans can only dream of.

In the 31 years he has worked at the tournament, Farrar says he has missed only one play day. The only reason he missed was it fell on the same day as his state board of dentistry exam. However, there was one other play day when he was able to play only nine holes. That particular day, also when he was in college, coincided with another test, although this one was far less important than the state boards. Unfortunately, even after explaining his opportunity, Farrar's professor would not let him take the exam another day.

"He was a real jerk," said a laughing Farrar. "Obviously he was not a golfer."

Farrar has had varying degrees of success playing the course. His low round is a 1-over par 73. He says he believes he has birdied every hole on the course except the difficult 455-yard, par 4 fifth, but he made up for that by making eagle at his hole, 13. Of course, that is from the member's tees, where the club tells players to play during their play day. But, Farrar says the club does not monitor every hole.

"I played 13 holes from the back tees one year to see what I could shoot," he said. "That day I shot 82, playing five holes from the members' tees. It's a whole different course from back there."

After playing nearly 30 rounds on the hallowed grounds, Farrar says the shock of having the privilege has worn off, but the experience never gets old.

"The first time you step on the tee... well, I just can't describe it," he said. "About the first six years I was there I just wanted to make contact with the ball. Those first couple of rounds I don't think I ever calmed down. To be able to be there is such an honor. It's awe inspiring."

NELSON LOOKING BACK ON OAKMONT, JUNE 17, 2007

Ten under par is the answer.

The question is what is the lowest score ever shot over the final 36 holes of the U.S. Open. But the person that shot rounds of 65 and 67 to break the record set in 1932 by Gene Sarazen is not named Tiger Woods, Phil Mickelson, Jack Nicklaus or Arnold Palmer. Rather, that distinction belongs to Marietta resident Larry Nelson.

The then-35-year-old Nelson used the two superb rounds and one of the most dramatic putts in Open history to defeat the then No. 1 player in the world and defending Open champion, Tom Watson, and win the 1983 U.S. Open at the site of this year's tournament — Oakmont Country Club — just outside of Pittsburgh.

Nelson, now 59, and a member of the Champions Tour, made an effort to get back to the site of the biggest victory of his career, but a pair of even-par 72s in sectional qualifying at Hawks Ridge Golf Club in Ball Ground left him outside the tournament field.

"To me (the record) is a big deal," Nelson said of his weekend play in '83. "When I broke it, it was a 51-year-old record and I don't think there's been another one that's been close. And it was different then. We used different equipment with the wooden club-heads, the old two-piece wound ball and the whole thing."

Odds are no one at Oakmont this week will threaten it either. Steve Stricker, who shot Saturday's low round of 68, would have to shoot 64 today to match it. The closest to the record for a winner since is Ray Floyd who won the Open three years after Nelson at Shinnecock Hills with closing rounds of 70-66.

But while Nelson played great on Saturday and Sunday, most people who remember his victory recall the 62-foot birdie putt that Monday morning.

The tournament was suspended Sunday afternoon when thunderstorms rolled through the hills of Western Pennsylvania. The leaders were in the middle of the back nine and tied at 4-under par. Nelson was through 15 holes and Watson was on the 14th green.

"We could see the storm move in and the sky got really black," Nelson said. "Then it rained so hard. We knew after about 30 minutes that we were not going back out there."

Most experts gave the No. 1 player in the world the advantage in the Monday finish and possible playoff, but of all people, Watson disagreed.

"In this situation now, I think Larry has the advantage," Watson told the New York Times that Sunday. "He's already through the (490-yard, par-4) 15th hole, but I have to get down in two on 14 and then I have to play 15, which is a tough hole. It is match play right now. He's up ahead of me and I'll have my eyes and ears open."

It did not take long Monday for Watson to hear a roar up ahead at the 16th hole.

Nelson's first shot of the day was a 4-wood on the 230-yard par-3. It was a shot he had practiced on the driving range before play began and he wanted to hit a slight fade into the right hand pin position. Instead, the shot went straight and the ball came to rest on the left edge of the green, more than 60 feet from the hole.

Ben Crenshaw has described the ensuing putt as "taking nearly 10 minutes" to reach the hole. The ball had to travel over two tiers with a 4-foot break and while it took no more than 10 seconds it was still too long for Nelson.

"I couldn't stay still," he said about watching the putt roll across the green. "By the time it went over the last tier and got to the last 20 feet I knew it had a chance. About 15 feet short of the hole it was right in the middle and I started walking. As it got closer I started running and it went right in."

For the first time during the tournament, Nelson held the U.S. Open lead. It was the exact opposite of how his week had started.

Nelson arrived at Oakmont that Monday only to find the airline had lost his golf clubs. He passed the time until his clubs arrived Tuesday afternoon using a borrowed putter to help get used to the lightning-fast Oakmont greens. And then, when his clubs did arrive, a variety of ailments limited his practice to only nine holes each Tuesday and Wednesday.

"We had played the PGA (Championship) there in '78. It had not changed much since then, so I knew the golf course," he said. "What I knew was I had to hit fairways and I knew what side of the pin I had to hit it on."

However, when Nelson began his tournament Thursday, he was nervous about what he saw lining the fairways and became more concerned about what he didn't see.

"The rough was high," he said about the course conditions during his opening-round 75. "Every time I looked down the fairway, all I could see was the rough. Then I couldn't see Seve's (Ballesteros) knees when he was standing over his ball in the rough. After that I decided I wasn't going to look down the fairway anymore. I started picking out a spot about 8 inches in front of my ball and lined myself up with that spot and hit my tee shot."

The adjustments worked. After his shaky opening round, Nelson shot 73 on Friday. His score of 6 over left him seven shots out of the lead, but he said his confidence really grew playing solid golf over his final nine holes, and by the weekend he had no trouble peering down the historic course's fairways.

"Larry is like 85 percent of the golfers out here," said Fuzzy Zoeller—who finished second to Nelson in the 1981 PGA Championship and would follow him as Open champion—at last month's Regions Charity Classic in Hoover, Ala. "We run very hot and cold. But when he got on it, was something to watch."

Everyone watched Saturday as Nelson posted a 6-under 65, the low round of the tournament. It was a round that included eight birdies, two bogeys and only 28 putts. His round moved him into a tie for third with Calvin Peete, one shot behind Watson and Masters champion Ballesteros.

On Sunday, Nelson and Watson quickly turned the tournament into a match play event. Nelson continued his hot play with a front-nine, 2-under 33. Unfortunately, he found himself further behind. Watson had made the turn in 31 opening a three-shot lead over his closest competitor.

"I shot 2-under and bogeyed No. 8," Nelson said. "I just felt like I had to keep doing the things I was doing. I think I shot 67 and (Watson) shot 69. It wasn't like he was playing awful. I think it may be the last Open where someone went out and won it."

Nelson pulled even on the 14th hole when he hit what he called his most important shot of the tournament, a pitching wedge to 1 1/2 feet to set up a gimmie birdie. Shortly after that the storm hit, suspending play and forcing the Monday finish. This time however, he had to sleep on the lead.

"I didn't do anything different Sunday night," he said. "I went back to the house and played Atari tennis with the boys. In fact I slept very well. I knew I was in control of what I was doing. Everything else would be left up to Tom."

After starting Monday with the monster birdie putt, Nelson finished his round with a three-putt bogey at the 18th. He was given a reprieve keeping his one shot lead when Watson missed a 6-foot par putt on 17.

Nelson watched Watson play the 18th hole with his wife, Gayle, from the scorer's tent. After a perfect drive, Watson's 8-iron approach sailed over the flag and over the green into the primary rough behind it. The misfire forced the defending champion to hole his chip shot if he expected to win the Open, something Nelson had seen him do the year before.

"I started having memories of 1982 when he chipped in (at No. 17 on Pebble Beach) to beat Nicklaus," Nelson said. "He had to make his chip, and for a while it got close to the hole, but it ended up 40-feet away."

While Nelson began to celebrate, Watson rolled in the long par putt. The result made little difference to the new champion, but it came as a shock to Gayle.

"I can remember looking at her," Nelson said. "I had to reassure her that I had still won the tournament. She thought he made that putt to tie me."

SCHNIEDERJANS SHOWING MENTAL EDGE BEYOND HIS YEARS, JUNE 9, 2011

At 17 years old, most teen-aged boys, when school lets out for the summer, are concentrating on sleep, figuring out which girl they are going to ask out and finding a part-time job.

They aren't worried about qualifying for the U.S. Open.

Ollie Schniederjans is no ordinary 17-year old.

He's no ordinary golfer either.

The Harrison High School graduate and future Georgia Tech golfer shot rounds of 66-68 at Hawks Ridge Golf Club on Monday in a U.S. Open sectional qualifier, the last step before our national tournament. He did it walking 36 holes over the 7,186-yard course, in 93-degree heat no less. He played his second round knowing he had a share of the tournament lead after the first 18 holes and he did it wondering if he had the mental game to play with the best players in the world.

As it turns out, Schniederjans likely won't be playing next week at Congressional Country Club outside Washington, D.C. His

10-under-par total earned him the second alternate's spot, when finishing 11-under might have gotten him into the tournament field.

Schniederjans' final score included a missed 1-foot putt on the par-5 fourth hole, the 13th hole of his afternoon round.

"It's the shortest putt I've ever missed in my life," Schniederjans said. "It was a fluke."

For his competitors, people following his group and the weekend golfer who may have heard about the missed putt, they are more likely jumping to one conclusion: He choked.

At that point, they might have said the pressure got to the young man, who graduated from Harrison six months early so he could join the Georgia Tech golf team for the spring semester.

When an average player plays too well and gets out of his comfort zone, the pressure will usually get to him or her. Not being used to the success, they might succumb to the moment, balance the birdies with more than enough bogies and end up shooting a round close to their norm.

The same can happen to a PGA Tour player. The television cameras show it all the time as a player trying to win his first tournament crumbles over the last few holes. And, instead of hoisting that trophy, that player is walking into the parking lot wondering what happened.

Some players never get over the collapse. Others come back stronger and learn to enjoy those pressure filled moments.

In this case, Schniederjans may look back when his playing days are through and say that missing the 1-footer was the best thing that ever happened to him.

Instead of watching his game crumble, Schniederjans played five holes of the gutsiest and smartest golf of his young life.

His first test was the 223-yard, par-3 fifth. Instead of rushing things or still worrying about his previous putt, he landed his tee shot 20-feet from the hole on his way to an easy two-putt par.

Then came the 319-yard, downhill par-4 sixth. It's a green that can be driven with a fairway wood and a hole where those in need of a birdie can count on making one.

Those were the same thoughts echoing in Schniederjans' head.

"I knew I needed a birdie on that hole," he said. "I played it too aggressive in my head."

Instead of a chance for birdie, Schniederjans had to manufacture a par. His 3-wood sailed into a group of low-hanging trees right of the green and right of the creek that guards it. His ball came to rest on a dense layer of soil and next to a cart path.

A lesser player would have tried the hero shot and focused on a short-sided pin, the kind of play that finds the putting surface once in a hundred tries. Instead, after listening to the good advice from his best friend and caddie, University of West Georgia golfer Matt Dyas, Schniederjans played away from the green and out of trouble.

"I knew it was the right play," Schniederjans said. "After hearing (Dyas') opinion, it meant a little bit more (to go that way). But it wasn't easy to do that."

Basing his Open hopes on his short game, Schniederjans was able to save par with a lob shot from 15 yards to 2 feet.

Taking advantage of a 310-yard drive on the 565-yard, par-5 seventh, he put what he called his best shot of the day, a 255-yard approach into the middle of the green for a two-putt birdie. He was now at 9-under.

After another big drive left him with a short approach into the 438-yard par-4 eighth, Schniederjans said he pulled a wedge shot for the first time all day. The ball came to rest 25 feet from the hole, 10 feet from the green and on a severe down slope.

His first thought was to chip the ball and he pulled the wedge from his bag. Then he thought better of it.

"A chip really wouldn't have made sense," he said. "If I hit 10 putts and 10 chips from there, my 10 putts are going to end up closer."

As the ball approached the hole, Schniederjans raised his putter above his head. When the ball found the bottom of the cup he gave a Tiger Woods-like fist-pump. He was 10-under.

"Coming into the day, I figured that 10 (under) would be the number, I really did," Schniederjans said. "Two years ago when they had (the sectional) here, 9 under went in without a playoff so I'd definitely thought 10 was going to make it."

More importantly, from the time he missed the 1-foot putt, he was 2-under par.

Heading to the final hole, Schniederjans said he was in a fog. He couldn't clear his head and was still fuzzy when he got over the ball to hit his tee shot on the 430-yard par 4.

"It was the most nervous I've ever felt over an easy tee shot," he said. "I almost backed off, but I didn't. I should have because I couldn't really focus."

He pulled his tee shot left into the trees and on a bed of pine straw. He had lost his chance for a closing birdie, but he got one more learning experience.

Schniederjans' pitch back to the fairway left him with a downhill lie and a shot of 80 yards to an elevated green. He hit the shot just like he wanted, but left himself with a 20-foot, downhill putt that broke about 5-feet.

Looking over the putt, Schniederjans said Dyas told him the one thing he waited his entire golfing life for.

"He told me, 'This is what you live for. It's the putt of your life.' Then, I hit (the putt) perfect."

The ball disappeared into the hole and, for a few minutes, it looked as if he may be on a plane to the nation's capital.

Hopefully, Schniederjans won't look back at that 1-foot putt and wonder "what if." He said he's not the kind of person to do that.

What Schniederjans learned on Monday was so much more. He learned he has the mental make up to play big-time golf.

Jack Nicklaus has always said playing when the pressure is highest is the fun part of golf. It's the reason you put in all the practice time, so a player can put themselves in that position.

Schniederjans now knows what the greatest player of all time is saying.

"That's the most pressure I've ever felt," he said. "People can criticize you for your mistakes, but they don't know what it's really like because they haven't been there."

Those are the people that will look at the short putt Schniederjans missed and say he blew a chance to make the Open.

What they actually missed was the beginning of a brilliant golf career.

OPEN CLOSED TO HISTORY, JUNE 19, 2007

Congratulations Angel Cabrera, you've won the U.S. Open. Now if you want to be remembered, go do it again, or at least win another four or five majors.

That doesn't seem fair considering Cabrera held off the No. 1 and No. 3 players in the world—Tiger Woods and Jim Furyk—to win our national championship at Oakmont Country Club—arguably the hardest golf course on the face of the planet to win his first major, but that's the same scenario that played out 24 years ago.

Larry Nelson shot rounds of 65-67 on the weekend in 1983 at the Western Pennsylvania jewel defeating the No. 1 player in the world at the time, Tom Watson, and the likely No. 2 player, Seve Ballesteros, but based on television coverage this weekend, hardly anyone would have known.

Nowhere during pre-tournament coverage on The Golf Channel was there mention of the Marietta resident. Highlight packages of Ben Hogan, Jack Nicklaus, Johnny Miller, and Ernie Els were prepared, but the unlikeliest champion of them all, Nelson, was bypassed. They didn't even show the 62-foot birdie putt Nelson made to take the lead during the final round.

One person who did notice the absence was the former champion.

"For one year I was the best player in the country," Nelson said last Thursday as the tournament was getting started. "I don't know how you don't acknowledge it and ignore it."

Nelson said he was going to call The Golf Channel just to find out why to satisfy his own curiosity. Those who watched the broadcast coverage on NBC did get to see the highlight once Furyk put his tee shot on the par-3 16th in roughly the same place on the green where Nelson holed his monster putt. But the bigger injustice is the fact Nelson wasn't there in person to try it again.

Unlike the other major championships that give lifetime exemptions for its former champions (the British Open allows former champions the option of playing until they turn 65) the United States Golf Association only gives its former champions the following 10 years, then they have to make the field through sectional qualifying—something the 59-year old Nelson, three-time major winner and World Golf Hall of Fame member is not fond of.

"The USGA hasn't been very proud of its champions," Nelson said. "The champions are not as important to them as the championship."

Or at least the less-popular ones; Nelson has never put himself out there as a controversial figure. He has never been a flamboyant player like a Ballesteros or a Greg Norman. And he has never been as colorful, as in clothing, as the late Payne Stewart. In fact, Nelson's most notable fashion statement may have come in the late '80s when he switched from a baseball-style cap to a Hogan poplin model. This does not and should not diminish the way the man played the game.

For this Open at Oakmont, Nelson should have been given a special exemption.

Ray Floyd was offered one for the 2004 Open at Shinnecock Hills. Why? Because that is where Floyd won his Open in 1986. In recent memory, Nick Price—who did not win an Open during his career—and Scott Simpson, far from the Who's Who of Golf, received a free pass.

Hale Irwin played the 1990 U.S. Open on an invitation by the USGA. All he did was win that year. Would Nelson have won this week at Oakmont? No, but he certainly would not have embarrassed himself.

The question of whether the thought of a special exemption was offered to Nelson floated around Hawks Ridge Golf Club three weeks ago when the Cherokee County course in Ball Ground hosted the sectional qualifier. A Georgia State Golf Association representative was overheard saying the USGA decided against the exemption because it wanted the strongest field possible.

That's probably the same reasoning they used in 2000 when they gave an exemption to the then 63-year old Jack Nicklaus at Pebble Beach or 13 years ago at Oakmont when they put then 63-year old Arnold Palmer in the field to play his last Open.

It's obvious both The Golf Channel and the USGA have selective memories, so if Cabrera wants to be remembered the next time the Open heads to Oakmont he's going to have to do a lot more winning. Or he will suffer the same unfortunate fate Nelson did this weekend.

GOLF'S 'KING' SHOWS SIGNS OF MORTALITY, APRIL 7, 2016

AUGUSTA—Thursday morning at Augusta National means the Masters begins with the honorary starters hitting ceremonial tee shots.

While the thousands of fans who lined the first fairway got to see six-time champion Jack Nicklaus and three-time winner Gary Player hit drives down the middle, it was obvious the crowd was there to see the only member of the "Big 3" who didn't have a club in his hand—Arnold Palmer.

The 86-year-old Palmer announced last month that he would not be actively participating in the ceremony because of a shoulder injury. Augusta National chairman Billy Payne said Wednesday he was looking forward to the four-time champion reprising his role in the future. On Thursday, Payne introduced Palmer by saying, "Not driving this year, but forever part of Masters tradition…"

Unfortunately, a return seems unlikely. "The King" appears frail, is walking with short, choppy steps and his balance is poor. He got help from Masters senior director Buzzy Johnson to get from the clubhouse to the tee, and then from Nicklaus and Player while taking photos. That's what made Thursday's appearance so important.

We may never see it again.

"I think he would have preferred to hit a golf ball," Nicklaus said. "I talked to him at the (Champions Dinner). I said, 'Arnold, when you're out there, what if we take you up and had you hit. I don't care if you putt it off the tee. I think everybody would love to have you do anything.'

"So, this morning, I talked to him and I said, 'What do you want to do? He said, 'I'm good.' I said, 'Fine, let's leave it alone.' I think it was probably the right thing."

Palmer was never just good. He was great.

He won 95 professional tournaments around the world, including seven majors. His prime coincided with the beginning of golf on TV, and he made it cool. And his coolness helped make the PGA Tour and the Masters what they are today.

"When he came on, and television came on, it was a mix made in heaven," former PGA and British Open champion Nick Price told the Augusta Chronicle. "Arnold Palmer, television and golf. Gary Player and Jack Nicklaus obviously did a lot, but it was Arnold who had that magnetism that brought everyone together."

Palmer rose to popularity by the way he played the game. His swing was unorthodox. He played out of the trees, he tried—and, more often than not, made—the hero shot, and he played his best while the pressure was on.

Palmer could have been in Hollywood. He had the looks to be a movie star and he played rounds of golf with the likes of President Dwight Eisenhower and Bob Hope, but he cemented his legacy as an American icon by being an everyman.

The pride of Latrobe, Pennsylvania, in the heart of steel country, Palmer was a guy who packed his lunchbox, hitched up his pants, puffed on his Pall Malls and put in a hard day's work. People could look at him and relate. They wanted to be like him and, in turn, Palmer brought the working-class people to the sport.

"He oozed charisma," Player said. "He was so charismatic and did so much for the game."

Not only did Palmer put the PGA Tour on its current path, but he did the same for the Champions Tour. His popularity jump-started the 50-and-over circuit when he came out to play in the early 1980s, and it has given older players an opportunity to make a living some 20 years longer than previous generations.

Lee Trevino once said every player on Tour should give half his winnings to Palmer because of what he meant to the game. It showed with how many of today's young players—including Rickie Fowler and Bryson DeChambeau, among others—came to the first tee Thursday—hours before their tee times—to watch the honorary starters' ceremony.

"That's a memory I'll never forget," said DeChambeau, a 22-year-old amateur who won the NCAA and U.S. Amateur titles last year. "It's not one I can fully describe just yet because it just happened a couple of hours ago. It's my first Masters. It's a special experience, but it's one I'll remember the rest of my life."

Palmer has been golf's greatest ambassador. He spent his life promoting the game, showing how it should be played and showing how someone should act while doing it.

Thursday may have been the final opportunity for the public to show Palmer what he meant to them. The fans responded by going eight- to 10-deep around No. 1 and they gave him an ovation that sounded like he had just made eagle on No. 15.

"To have longevity has been a special gift," the 80-year-old Player said. "And to come here today and be on the tee with Arnold being a part of us, it was gratifying and sad, because everything shall pass."

BRIAN KATREK, VOICE OF KENNESAW STATE BROADCASTS, CALLING THE MASTERS, APRIL 9, 2019

AUGUSTA — Golf fans who watch the Masters on CBS know that Jim Nantz and Nick Faldo will be calling the action in the 18th tower.

What they do not know is the voice of the Kennesaw State Owls will be up there with them.

Brian Katrek, the play-by-play voice for the Owls' football and basketball teams during local TV and ESPN-streamed broadcasts, will be one of two hosts calling the golf action on the final hole for PGA Tour Radio, which can be heard on Sirius XM. He will be in the tower with color commentator Charlie Rymer for the first two-plus hours of each day's coverage.

Katrek, a Cobb County native and Sprayberry High School graduate, will move to the tower at Nos. 15 and 16 to call two of the most exciting holes in golf for the remainder of the broadcast, when Mike Tirico comes in following his Golf Channel duties.

It marks the 18th time Katrek will be broadcasting the Masters, but the first time in a decade that he has spent any time in the premier chair at No. 18.

"I've spent time in every tower they've had," Katrek said.

For the last 22 years, Katrek has called golf on radio in one form or another, but when he started, he did not play the sport, let alone know much about it.

"I was working at 790 the Zone," Katrek said of the Atlanta-area sports radio station. "One of our sales guys came in and said a sponsor wanted to pay for a golf show, so we were going to have a golf show. Then, they started asking who wanted to do it. I raised my hand."

Katrek learned about the sport quickly. His father-in-law was a golfer and got him started in the game, and Katrek took almost daily lessons at TPC Sugarloaf in Duluth. Now, he is a near scratch player.

The experience has helped Katrek in every step of his career, from the first golf show on 790 the Zone when he was still a freshman at Kennesaw State, to his current daily talk show—"Katrek and Maginnes on Tap"—with John Maginnes from 5-7 p.m. on PGA Tour Radio.

"Katrek and Maginnes on Tap," with its national audience, is considered to be the most listened-to golf talk show in the world, and it is a platform Katrek does not take for granted.

"It's fantastic because of the golf community," said Katrek, who also hosts The Golf Show on 680 the Fan on Sundays at 9 a.m. "I'm talking to people I know, whether I've met them or not. They know us whether they've met us or not. We all talk in a common language."

Also included on Katrek's resume is his broadcasting work at the U.S. Open, PGA Championship, Ryder Cup and Presidents Cup, as well as another dozen PGA Tour events each year. He is also the anchor of the Emmy Award-winning "Live @" webcast on PGATour.com.

"I know way more about the Valero Texas Open than anyone really should," he said.

Katrek has also seen a lot of good golf at Augusta National. Like

CBS, PGA Tour Radio works on a year-to-year contract with the club, so he never knows for sure if he is going to get the call to go back.

Still, each year coming through the gates feels like the first.

"'Special' is the word everyone uses," Katrek said, "and that's what it is."

One of Katrek's favorite moments came when he was calling the action at No. 16 in 2016. With the hole in its traditional Sunday location, Katrek watched Shane Lowry, Davis Love III and Louis Oosthuizen all make holes-in-one. The final one came when Oosthuizen's ball knocked J.B. Holmes' ball out of the way and then continued to roll to the cup.

"Thank goodness I could tell which ball it was," Katrek said. "I was using binoculars, so I could see what ball it was. If J.B. Holmes' ball goes in, everyone still would have thought it would have been a hole-in-one, but it would have been a couple of 2s.

"You know how, when there are roars in one area of the course, the people want to go be part of it? I've been in that tower for a lot of years and that was the most festive I've ever seen it. It was a party down there."

With most of the top players in good form heading into the tournament, Katrek is not sure what he will see this week. All he knows is that it likely will be good. It is the same way he looks at every week on tour, and he hopes it does not end any time soon.

"I'll do this job as long as they'll have me," Katrek said. "I'd like to do it another 30 years. I hope this is the last job I ever have."

OLLIE IS ARROGANT, AND THAT'S A GOOD THING, MAY 25, 2014

ATLANTA—Ollie Schniederjans is arrogant.

After sitting with him for more than an hour a couple of weeks ago to do an in-depth interview, it was clear that there were two stories to tell.

The first was about the success a mild-mannered young man from

Harrison High School was having as a member of the Georgia Tech golf program. The second was about his off-the-charts level of confidence, but the latter I had no idea how I was going to convey without making it sound like Schniederjans was conceited.

That was until I heard what Golf Channel analyst Brandel Chamblee had to say to the crowd at the Ben Hogan Award banquet Sunday.

Schniederjans was one of three finalists for the award annually given to the nation's best college golfer. But before the award presentation, Chamblee was asked what Schniederjans and the other collegiate players in attendance could expect if and when they finally arrive on the PGA Tour.

"The players that make it — there's no other way to say it — are arrogant," said Chamblee, a former PGA journeyman. "Now, you can be arrogant and likeable, but you have to be arrogant. You have to have an unbelievable amount of belief to go with that talent."

That is Schniederjans to a tee and here are a couple of examples to prove the point.

In eight days, he will play at a U.S. Open sectional tournament in Roswell. History says there will be three players from that event that will advance to the U.S. Open at Pinehurst.

Schniederjans fully expects to be one of those three.

"I know I'm going to have to shoot a really low score," said Schniederjans, who shot rounds of 71-65 and is tied for sixth at 4-under par heading into today's third round of the NCAA championships. "But I am so capable of that here in Georgia. Any time I play in this area — if I have to go shoot 11-under, then I'll just go and do it.

"I've done it so many times. When I'm practicing, I'm looking at hitting it dead straight at my target every time. If I do that all day, I'm going to have 15 or 16 real good birdie chances and I'm a great putter, so I'll make five or six or seven of them."

There was a time I was a very good player. If I shot 76 it was a bad day, but there is no way I could ever fathom the mindset it takes to know that shooting 11-under par is no more a problem than rolling out of bed in the morning.

But there was no bragging in his voice. It wasn't trash talk. He was just stating what he considers to be a fact.

And then there's this. Schniederjans has actually been in that position before. In 2011, after his junior year of high school, he was in the mix for one of the three qualifying spots when the sectional was held at Hawks Ridge in Ball Ground.

He had a share of the lead after shooting 66 in the morning, and Schniederjans was 2-under on his second 18 when he reached the par-5 fourth, the 13th hole of his round. After hitting his second shot into a greenside bunker, he blasted his third shot to within a foot of the hole, but instead of a tap-in birdie, he missed the putt.

Instead of dreading on that moment, Schniederjans played the last five holes 2-under par. He went on to finish one shot out of a playoff for the third and final qualifying spot.

When I asked him what he remembers about that moment, it should be no surprise.

It wasn't the putt.

"I actually completely forgot that I missed that 1-footer," he said. "Whenever I think about that, I think about the two 20-footers I made on the last two holes. I really, honestly, did kind of forget about that 1-footer. I think it was a bit of a fluke, but the way I refocused and played hard coming in is what I remember. I'm not easily flappable."

Schniederjans has won five tournaments this year and has finished outside the top 12 only once in 14 events.

He's going to represent the U.S. in England at next month's Palmer Cup, and he's got his sights on playing in the U.S. Open, British Open, U.S. Amateur and next year's Masters.

Not bad for being only three years removed from playing his home matches in west Cobb at Brookstone Golf and Country Club.

As I continued to listen to Chamblee address the Hogan Award banquet attendees, he reminded Schniederjans and the other finalists that, regardless of what they do going forward, they have already achieved more in the game of golf than only a fraction of a percent of players ever will.

But that would never be enough for the Powder Springs native.

Chamblee's words about the players needing to be arrogant reminded me of a quote that was once offered about the greatest golfer in the history of the game, Jack Nicklaus.

"He was so good." Former PGA player J.C. Snead said, "When you go head-to-head against Nicklaus, he knows he's going to beat you, you know he's going to beat you, and he knows you know he's going to beat you."

Nicklaus wasn't the kind of player who disrespected an opponent. He knew he was good and let his clubs do his talking.

That's the way Schniederjans is playing in the collegiate ranks right now.

I'm anxious to see what's next.

TWENTY YEARS LATER, O'MEARA'S IMPROBABLE TITLE STILL RESONATES, APRIL 6, 2018

AUGUSTA—There was an anticipation for the 2018 Masters to potentially be one of the greatest in history.

At the midway point, it doesn't seem to be disappointing. The leaderboard is packed with top players like Patrick Reed, Rory McIlroy and Jordan Spieth. It will be interesting when we look back on it in 20 years... how will it be remembered.

Looking back at the 1998 Masters, it is safe to say it is one of the most unlikely to have ever happened. From an amateur from Georgia Tech announcing his presence on the big stage to a certain 58-year-old six-time champion making a final run, to the eventual champion—it may have been one of the most entertaining and unexpected Masters ever played.

The amateur was Matt Kuchar, then a 19-year-old sophomore business major with the Yellow Jackets, who shot rounds of 72-76-68-72 and finished in a tie for 21st. With an engaging smile and plenty of game, Kuchar quickly endeared himself to the Augusta National fans.

When Bobby Jones created the Masters, a big part of the tournament was always amateur golf, and Kuchar, who has since won seven times on the PGA Tour, including the Players Championship, embraced the moment to its fullest. The event, like with most players, has become close to his heart, and it has never wavered.

"It's so exciting to be at the Masters, so exciting," Kuchar said. "Every year, I come looking forward to this week and, every year, you get such a buzz on the driving range, in the practice rounds, that you can't wait for golf to get going.

"It's hard to believe (it's been 20 years). I thought back to walking up 18 with my dad on the bag and you remember each day, kind of going, 'How special is this?' I kind of felt that (Thursday), just as the shadows were long and late in the afternoon, so I thought back to '98 and walking up with my dad."

Like Kuchar, Jack Nicklaus first came to Augusta as an amateur. Jones said Nicklaus played a game with which he was not familiar. Nicklaus then proved Jones right by becoming the tournament's greatest champion.

Earlier that week in 1998, Nicklaus—12 years since his last victory in 1986—was presented with a plaque on the course, which is now located between the 16th and 17th holes. During the presentation, tournament chairman Jack Stephens spoke about the six victories listed on the plaque, but, just in case something else historic happened, Stephens added, "We left a little room at the bottom."

That may have been foreshadowing as the "Golden Bear" proved he could still growl. He started his final round with birdies on four of his first seven holes to pull within two shots of the lead.

He was still two back when he looked over a 12-foot putt for birdie on 16.

Unfortunately, for what seemed like the only time of his career at Augusta National, when he needed to make a putt on No. 16, he didn't. A huge groan went through the Georgia pines. Nicklaus parred in, shot 68 and finished sixth.

"Well, I played the tournament on one leg," Nicklaus told Golfweek Magazine this week. "I had my hip replaced nine months later. I could still walk, but wasn't very good. I don't remember much about the tournament. I couldn't tell you what score I shot. All I do remember is (my son) Steve caddied for me. I got to the 15th hole, and I looked at Steve and I said, 'Steve, if we finish the same way I finished in '86, we're going to win this golf tournament.' I didn't. We didn't win.

"What did I finish, sixth? Yeah. It was OK for an old guy."

That left six of the top 10 players in the world—including No. 1 Tiger Woods, who had won the Masters by 12 shots the previous year, and No. 2 Ernie Els—in contention to win the tournament.

Heading into the '98 Masters, Mark O'Meara, who was ranked 14th, was on the short list of best players never to win a major. He had won the U.S. Amateur and figured out how to win at Pebble Beach five times, but he never seemed to get over the last hurdle to becoming a major champion.

O'Meara started the final round two shots behind 1992 champion Fred Couples, but the battle was soon joined by another former Georgia Tech standout, David Duval, the 10th-ranked player in the world.

By the time O'Meara birdied the 15th hole, he was two behind Duval and one back of Couples.

It set the stage for something that hadn't happened in 40 years.

At that time, the last person to birdie the 17th and 18th holes to win the Masters was Arnold Palmer in 1958.

O'Meara now had that chance, but it seemed like he may have been the only one that knew it.

"It was a tournament where you were never thinking Mark was going to win and then he did," said ESPN's Scott Van Pelt, who, at the time, was an anchor at Golf Channel. "All day, it looked like you were looking elsewhere—Fred Couples, David Duval—even Jim Nantz, it was like all of a sudden it hit him: 'Oh my, Mark O'Meara has a putt to win the Masters.'"

After making a birdie on 17, O'Meara had a 20-foot putt from right of the hole on 18 to win. Historically, it was a putt no one ever seemed to make.

Only, this time, O'Meara did.

"I don't think anyone expected me to win," he said. "I was just as shocked, and if you look at my face on the video, I'm looking like, what just happened?"

At the award ceremony, the then-41-year-old had his green jacket presented to him by the 22-year-old Woods, who considered O'Meara a big brother figure. O'Meara said, as he was putting the jacket on, Woods whispered in his ear, "You deserve this."

The leaderboard bared that out.

Fourteen of the top 16 finishers, including the top nine, went on to win at least one major championship. The list included Jim Furyk finishing fourth, Paul Azinger fifth, Woods eighth, Phil Mickelson in a tie for 12th and Els in a tie for 16th. Overall, the top 23 players eventually combined to collect 54 major titles, and O'Meara added his second later that summer by winning the British Open at Royal Birkdale.

On Friday, O'Meara announced that this year's Masters would be his last. The last time he made the cut was 2015, and now at 61 years old and after rounds of 78 and 81, he said it's time for him to leave.

"It's a big golf course for me nowadays," O'Meara said "You've got kids out here regularly hitting it 315 (yards), and I'm hitting it 265. That makes it awfully tough to compete."

O'Meara also said he doesn't want to come out and shoot 78, 79 or 80, just to be out there playing. He said he's not one of the legends, like Tom Watson or Jack Nicklaus, who the fans clamor to see.

"I'm just a guy," O'Meara said.

He's just a guy that was the most unlikely winner of what was one of the most unlikely Masters in history.

MARIETTA SURGEON HEADING TO AMEN CORNER TO WATCH HIS 51ST MASTERS, APRIL 11, 2013

In 1963, Jack Nicklaus won the first of his six Masters tournaments at Augusta National Golf Club.

Dr. Tony Musarra was there to see it.

Nicklaus went on to win six green jackets, and Musarra was there to see them all.

Musarra also saw Arnold Palmer win his last title in 1964, then watched Tiger Woods win four, and Phil Mickelson and Nick Faldo win three each.

But Musarra, a plastic surgeon at the Plastic Surgery Center of the South in Marietta, wasn't just at those Masters tournaments. Since 1963, he has been at every Masters.

From the time he was an undergraduate student at the University of Georgia, Musarra has made the trek to golf's first major tournament of the season. And this year, he will make his 51st consecutive trip to Amen Corner.

In that time, Musarra has seen almost every great player of the game, and he's been on hand to see significant culture change. He was there in 1975 when Augusta National Golf Club allowed Lee Elder to become the first black player to compete in the tournament. And this year, he may have the opportunity to see the club's first two female members—former Secretary of State Condoleezza Rice and financier Darla Moore—wearing their green jackets.

"We were happy to see the first black player," said Musarra, who added that if there were any racial incidents around Elder, Musarra didn't see them. "The crowd was very respectful."

He's also seen the course itself change with the times and the evolving golf club technology. Musarra was there when Augusta National changed from Bermuda grass greens to bent grass in the early 1980s, and he's seen it lengthened from 6,800 yards to nearly 7,500 to keep up with the ever-increasing driving lengths of Woods, John Daly and Rory McIlroy.

Musarra also had a chance to meet many of the game's greats.

"I met Jack Nicklaus," he said. "He's very nice and very friendly."

He's also had the chance to meet Tom Watson, Ray Floyd, Hubert Green, Gary Player, Ben Crenshaw and his favorite player—Palmer.

For the 69-year-old Musarra, a 1961 Marietta High School graduate and former football player for legendary Blue Devils coach French Johnson, he said he understands the historical significance of the things he's seen within Augusta National's gates.

"I do think about it," Musarra said. "I've had an opportunity and the privilege to watch the very best play the game of golf and see (Augusta National's) place in the world."

On Spring Break

Of course, Musarra didn't always feel that way. His annual journey to the Masters didn't originally begin just to see the greats of the game, or because he loved the game of golf. That would come later for the Marietta Country Club member who holds a 16 handicap.

Musarra's first trip came when he was a student at Georgia and the Masters happened to coincide with spring break. One day, he said he was walking through his Kappa Sigma fraternity house and saw a stack of forms to apply for tournament tickets. It was then when Musarra decided that Augusta would be where he and his fraternity brothers would spend their vacation.

"We got 16 tickets," he said. "We had so many, we couldn't give them away."

Once he was there, Musarra said he was drawn to Palmer, arguably the most popular player in Masters history, because of his charisma and aggressive style of play.

Musarra said his favorite Masters was the second he attended, when Palmer won his fourth green jacket and the final major of his career in 1964. Palmer shot 12-under par and beat Nicklaus, the defending champion at the time, by six shots. Player and Billy Casper, the other top players of the day, also finished the tournament in the top five.

"I loved Arnold Palmer," Musarra said. "Arnie's Army was always the best following group.

"Nicklaus always had good cheers, but you could always tell a Palmer roar. It was more of a shrill."

Nicklaus was just becoming the player that would dominate Augusta National and the PGA Tour at that time and, to many of the golf fans—including Musarra and his fraternity brothers—Nicklaus was still known as "Fat Jack."

But by the time Nicklaus had won five green jackets and 17 major titles, Musarra had grown to cheer for him, too. It's why 1986 also ranks at the top of his memory list.

Nicklaus was 46 years old and had not won a major in six years, or a regular tour event in two, heading into that tournament. But with a final-round 65, and a back nine of 30, he turned back the clock to win his sixth Masters.

"We had all come to respect him so much," Musarra said of Nicklaus holding off the likes of Greg Norman, Seve Ballesteros and Tom Kite on that Sunday. "It was very moving to me. It was a very emotional thing to see."

Considering that the 1986 Masters is considered the greatest in the 76-year history of the tournament, it would have been a shame if Musarra would have missed it, but his five-decade long string of Masters nearly ended before it really got started.

"During my third year at Georgia, someone took my ticket and made copies of it," Musarra said. "Some of those people (using counterfeit tickets) got rowdy and had their tickets confiscated and the club traced the number back to me."

Augusta National officials are notoriously strict when it comes to patron conduct, and if a person is found to have broken the rules, it's not uncommon for the club to take away the offending patron's tickets permanently.

"I got called into the Dean's office (at Georgia) with the security people, and I was thoroughly questioned for more than 2 and a half hours," Musarra said. "They didn't believe me at first (that I had nothing to do with it). I was sweating, but I never changed my story. I guess they finally just believed me and let me go. I think (that incident is) what led to tickets becoming more sophisticated."

Musarra no longer has 16 tickets. Over the years, the tournament slowly curtailed how many each person is allowed to purchase, but when Musarra did have larger amounts, he took the opportunity to bring friends, family and colleagues to experience the things he looks forward to every spring.

The Joy Of Sharing

The current limit for badges is four per patron. But while the numbers of friends and relatives Musarra can take has decreased, the joy he gets from taking someone to Augusta for the first time never fades.

"It's always such a pleasure to do it," he said. "For people that haven't seen (Augusta), it's always great to be able to share in letting them see it for the first time."

With more than 50 years of watching the Masters, Musarra has developed a routine for seeing some of the best golf on the course.

"I start off at No. 2 green," he said. "There, you can see play on Nos. 2, 3, 7, and there is a big scoreboard. From No. 2, I'll go to No. 9, and then I'll walk down to No. 13, and then 16.

"Sixteen is always in my heart."

The par-3 will always be special to Musarra because that is where he and the large contingent from Georgia would sit every spring, root for Palmer and razz Nicklaus. He and his friends would sit on the large mound that is left of the green and watch group after group come through.

On those first visits, No. 16 was where the party was most likely to break out.

"The first few years I was there, the club would allow us to bring coolers in," Musarra said. "It could get a little rowdy down there. I think the rules may have changed because of the college kids."

Musarra said his routine of starting at No. 2 and eventually arriving at No. 16 has allowed him to see some of the greatest shots in the history of golf, and two recent shots are right at the top of his list.

In 2005, Woods came to No. 16 in the final round trying to hold off a charging Chris DiMarco.

Woods' tee shot finished over the green and left him with a chip shot that he could not play toward the hole if he had any hopes to make a par. He had to chip into the slope of the green and let the contour bring the ball back to the cup.

The chip shot did exactly that, and instantly became a Nike

commercial when the ball hovered over the hole with the "swoosh" on the ball in plain view of the camera, before falling in the hole for a birdie.

Musarra had a slightly different view of the shot.

"I was on the other side of the pond," he said. "I was 30 yards away. There was an absolutely huge crowd, and I was sitting directly behind the hole on the other side of the pond."

For Musarra's other favorite shot, he was a lot closer.

In 2010, Mickelson had the lead on Sunday as he came to the par-5 13th hole. He hit his drive through the fairway and into the pines that line the right side of the hole, and Musarra was one of the first to get near where Mickelson's ball came to rest.

"The key to getting in position is to stand right at the rope," he said. "When the marshal clears the area, he will take the rope down, and if you are there, you are going to be right next to the player."

Musarra found himself less than 15 feet from Mickelson as he conferred with his caddie and decided how to play his second shot off pine straw, through what couldn't have been much more than a 5-foot gap in the trees, which were about 10 feet in front of him.

"First, he took out a lofted club like he was going to lay up," Musarra said. "But then he changed to (a 6-iron).

"I thought, 'Surely, he's not going to do this.'"

Mickelson hit his second shot, avoided the trouble and watched as the ball landed on the front of the green and stopped 6 feet from the hole.

"He had to come out from under the tree limbs to see (the shot)," Musarra said, "but you could tell he liked it. He pumped his fist and was very demonstrative."

Musarra said he was amazed at what he had just seen, and it was that kind of shot that has drawn him to Mickelson as one of his favorite current-day players. It may also be because Mickelson's style of play reminds him so much of Palmer.

"He's a pretty aggressive player," Musarra said. "He likes to charge ahead and try riskier shots. Palmer's my all-time favorite, but I like Mickelson for those same reasons."

As he has gotten older, Musarra has cut back on the number of days he attends each year. From 1963 until 1978, he never missed a day. This year, he plans on being there for the final two rounds.

Nothing Better To Do

Amazingly, in 51 years, he has never come close to missing a tournament.

"From time to time, I've thought there may be something better to do with that weekend," he said. "But each time, I've decided to go, and I've always had the same enthusiasm."

Augusta National was contacted about Musarra's patron streak, but there was no response as to whether his story is unique.

"I can't imagine many others that could have gone to as many in a row as me," he said. "There may have been people that have gone to as many, but not in a row."

Despite attending 50 straight Masters, Musarra said he has never had the opportunity to play the golf course, although he hopes to one day.

He also said he doesn't have a number in mind as to how many Masters he hopes to attend, and he's not likely to know how long the streak will reach.

There's one reason for that.

"I'll probably go until I die," Musarra said.

STEWART'S MEMORY LIVES ON IN AUGUSTA, APRIL 12, 2014

AUGUSTA—The Masters and Augusta National Golf Club are synonymous with the city of Augusta.

But drive downtown and you find a small part of the city dedicated to the Ryder Cup.

There, over Bill's Place, a liquor store on the corner of 5th Street and Broad Street—just two blocks from the Savannah River and only 5 miles from Amen Corner—there's a mural of the 1999 U.S. Ryder Cup team that stretches the length of the building.

One of the focal points of the painting is a profile of the late Payne Stewart.

It was out of respect that Bill Prince, owner of the package store, decided to commemorate the team and pay homage to the three-time major champion, who tragically died at the age of 42 in a plane crash, only weeks after the American team's near impossible rally at the Country Club in Brookline, Mass. Prince did so through the artistic impression of locally renowned artist William Fahnoe.

"He usually painted one for me every four or five years," said Prince, who added that Augusta native Larry Mize had come to his store to see a mural Fahnoe had done of Mize's famous chip-in to win the 1987 Masters. "This time, I wanted to commemorate Payne Stewart and the great comeback victory of the Ryder Cup team. It was only a few weeks after that (Stewart) was dead."

The mural is done in four segments.

From left to right, it depicts the players running onto the 17th green to celebrate after Justin Leonard made a dramatic 45-foot putt to seal the victory, a large image of the Ryder Cup trophy, and then two rows of portraits depicting Stewart, the other 11 players on the American team that year—Leonard, David Duval, Jim Furyk, Tom Lehman, Davis

Love III, Jeff Maggert, Phil Mickelson, Mark O'Meara, Steve Pate, Hal Sutton and Tiger Woods—and captain Ben Crenshaw.

Ironically, the current mural replaced one depicting Augusta National co-designer and President in Perpetuity Bobby Jones, which Fahnoe had painted four years earlier. The change was something Prince said he had no second thoughts about doing.

"All the players in the mural are still connected to the Masters," he said.

That's true. Crenshaw, Mickelson, O'Meara and Woods have won the tournament, and the others had all played in the event. But since Stewart was the main inspiration for the mural, you can't help but begin to wonder what he would have looked like dressed as a Masters champion.

If you close your eyes it's an easy sight to imagine—Stewart dressed in his traditional plus-fours or knickers, probably in a soft yellow or beige with the matching Ivy hat, all wrapped in a green jacket.

"It would have been nice," O'Meara said with a great big smile and a laugh. "It would have been so nice."

Stewart didn't have the best Masters record, but he was competitive. His best showings came when he finished eighth in 1986 and ninth in 1993.

To that point, they were his only top-10 finishes, but Stewart arguably played the best golf of his career in 1999. While he could only muster a tie for 52nd that spring in Augusta, he won at Pebble Beach early in the season and the U.S. Open that summer. It was good enough to win more than $2 million, and he finished seventh on the money list.

With his free-flowing golf swing and superb iron play, it would be nice to know how golf history would have changed if Stewart had four or five more years of his prime, and a handful more trips down Magnolia Lane.

O'Meara thinks Stewart would have had a good chance to win.

"To play here, you have to have imagination and great touch," he said. "Payne had that.

"He would have been a great champion and a welcome member to the club. He meant a lot to golf and we all miss him."

Despite it nearing the 15th anniversary of Stewart's death and the "Miracle at Brookline," Prince said the mural is still in good shape and there for all to see. The only things different are the colors, which have faded thanks to the beating they take in the afternoon sun, but he refuses to redo it out of respect for Fahnoe, who passed away in 2009.

However, Prince did add there may be one way he could consider changing the mural.

"Well, I'm definitely not planning on taking it down tomorrow," Prince said. "But if Larry Mize should win the Masters again, I might have to think about putting him back on the wall."

Considering Mize is 55 years old and past his competitive prime, Stewart and the 1999 Ryder Cup team should have their place overlooking downtown Augusta for a long time to come.

SPACIOUS NEW MERCHANDISE BUILDING A ONE-STOP SHOP FOR ALL THINGS AUGUSTA NATIONAL, APRIL 2, 2018

AUGUSTA—Just inside the gates of Augusta National Golf Club sits what could be the single largest tourist attraction this side of the Mississippi.

No, it's not the famed Amen Corner—holes Nos. 11-13 on the back nine.

It's not Magnolia Lane either.

It's the Masters merchandise building.

Make that the new-and-improved, state-of-the-art, Masters merchandise building.

For those who have been to the tournament before, the majority of the new building sits where the old building used to be. However, it is now at least twice the size of its predecessor.

For those who have not been to the tournament, the new building is probably 30,000 square feet of retail space, with 2,000 people armed with Visa cards crammed into it at any given moment.

When the club built the reportedly $50 million press center at the back of the driving range last year, the old two-story press building that sat next to the first fairway was reconfigured.

The bottom level of the old building has become a new concession area with more seating and better restroom facilities.

The top level became part of the new pro shop.

As you enter the shop, it gives off a museum-type feel. While people are in line, you have the opportunity to learn about Drive, Chip and Putt tournament, the Latin America Amateur Championship and the Asia Pacific Amateur Championship.

The first event brings junior golfers to the club to compete for national championships the Sunday before the Masters. The latter two were organized with the help of Augusta National, and the winners earn invitations to play in the year's first major.

There are also digital signatures and quotes of former Masters champions, along with large pieces of artwork from tournaments past.

While all that is great, it doesn't distract from the moment at hand—that people are willing to spend just about anything for items with a Masters logo. The fact that they can only get it on site, and this one week of the year, allows them to justify the likely enormous amount of money they are about to spend on a unique variety of items.

Need a garden gnome dressed as an Augusta National caddie? You can get one here. Need Masters boxer shorts, sunglasses, binoculars, coffee mugs, glassware or neckties?

How about a new leash and bowl for man's best friend? Or, maybe a fashionable green dog collar. I know it looks good, because they had it on a mannequin of a dog, which was one of 385 mannequins in use.

Want the new and hot item this year? Get the needlepoint wallets of the clubhouse and Amen Corner.

By far, though, the most popular items in the merchandise shop are the hats and shirts. The problem is figuring out which one(s) to buy.

Want a traditional ball cap, visor or bucket hat? There are 125 to choose from in every color and style.

What kind of shirt do you want? Dress shirt, golf shirt, T-shirt — long- and short-sleeve — pullover, vest, sweater and jackets — every color, every style and all with the outline of the United States of America with a flagstick planted firmly in Augusta, Georgia.

And if that isn't enough, heading to one of the 64 checkout areas, you have to pass all the impulse items that can force you to have to take out a second mortgage.

Signs, golf balls, towels. Watches, posters, playing cards. Calendars, flags, tumblers.

And that still doesn't even begin to scratch the surface. To make matters worse, the attendants hand you a shopping bag as you walk in, and from what I could see, most people were filling them up.

I know how much I spent, and I feel like I got off light. The people standing behind me had a total just shy of $500. The people ahead of me had to have cleared at least $1,000.

Last year, when Sergio Garcia won the Masters, he earned a first-place check of $1,980,000. Based on the sales I saw in the pro shop, Augusta National made that back by lunchtime Monday.

Buying Masters gear, a tradition unlike any other.

SCHNIEDERJANS CLOSES AMATEUR CAREER
WITH TIE FOR 12TH AT BRITISH OPEN,
JULY 21, 2015

At 7:40 a.m. Monday, the name Ollie Schniederjans was trending on Twitter.

People across the world were taking notice as the Powder Springs native took advantage of the benign conditions and shot up the leaderboard at St. Andrews in the final round of the 144th British Open.

Schniederjans began the day with birdies on the first two holes, made a bogey on No. 3, and then proceeded to make birdies on four of the next five holes, including a 30-footer on No. 9, to make the turn in 31. After he drove the 340-yard par 4 10th hole and two putted for birdie, the former Harrison High School and Georgia Tech standout was 10-under par, tied for fifth and two shots off the lead.

"Amazing final day," Schniederjans told the Golf Channel. "Couldn't ask for anything more special, feeling like I belonged out here and watching my name go up the leaderboard."

Schniederjans had remained an amateur through this week because he had earned exemptions into last month's U.S. Open and for this week's trip to the Old Course by earning the Mark McCormack medal by closing last season as the top-ranked amateur in the world.

He finished tied for 42nd at Chambers Bay in the first major of his career. Then, on Friday, after shooting 70-72 the first two rounds in Scotland, he joined only Phil Mickelson (1991) and Tiger Woods (1996) as the only amateurs over the last 50 years to make the cut in both opens in the same year.

Schniederjans followed with another 70 in Sunday's third round to get to 4-under par, but he felt he left a lot of shots on the course because his putter let him down—something that doesn't happen very often.

"When I'm practicing, I'm looking at hitting it dead straight at my target every time," he said at the end of his junior season at Tech. "If I do that all day, I'm going to have 15 or 16 real good birdie chances and I'm a great putter, so I'll make five or six or seven of them."

In his final round as an amateur Monday, Schniederjans proved to be correct, and for a while, it appeared as if he was going to post a number the leaders would have to look at throughout the round.

He was still 10-under when he reached the "Road Hole," St. Andrews' famous 17th. Schniederjans watched as Phil Mickelson, who was also 10-under and playing in the group ahead of him, hooked his tee shot over the edge of the Old Course Hotel and onto one of the balconies of its many suites.

Schniederjans didn't say whether the sight of Mickelson's shot had any effect on his thinking, but there may have been a residual effect. Schniederjans hit his worst tee shot of the week and then followed it with an even worse pull-hook into the grandstand between the green and No. 2 tee. After wedging it to the front of the green, Schniederjans three putted for double bogey.

It ended any dream he may have had at winning the tournament. It also ended up costing Schniederjans a chance at low-amateur.

"On 17, I just screwed up," he said.

That left Schniederjans one hole left in his amateur career. And if you are going to bring any career to a close—see Arnold Palmer, Jack Nicklaus and Tom Watson standing on the Swilcan Bridge—there's not a better place than the 18th hole at St. Andrews.

Schniederjans powered a drive to just short of the "Valley of Sin," a large swale in front of the green. He bumped a wedge shot into the face of the slope, the ball took one hop and made an abrupt stop a little more than 2 feet from the hole. It was a classy way to close, and it was appreciated by the thousands of spectators watching from the grandstands.

"The 18th was great," Schniederjans said. "The last hole as an amateur, it was special for sure."

When he made the birdie putt, he had shot 67, was 9-under par, had posted the lowest score ever shot by an amateur in the Open championship and was the leader in the clubhouse.

Unfortunately, those marks would fall a few hours later. Oklahoma State's Jordan Niebrugge claimed low amateur at 11-under, and Schniederjans finished the tournament tied for 12th, six shots behind Zach Johnson's winning score of 15-under, but that wouldn't tarnish the day. Schniederjans finished tied with players like former World No. 1 Luke Donald and 2014 U.S. Open champion Martin Kaymer, and he would finish two shots ahead of former Open champions Mickelson, fellow Georgia Tech alum Stewart Cink and Padraig Harrington.

Schniederjans started playing the game at age 12. He advanced through local U.S. Open qualifying for the first time at 14 and made it to the No. 1 amateur in the world by 20. Now at 22, Schniederjans is ready for his next challenge, and said so in a pair of tweets after his round on Monday.

"Very special way to finish my amateur career today at @TheHomeofGolf in the @TheOpen. Thanks everyone for the nice messages and support!" he said. "On to @RBCCanadianOpen as a pro!"

Schniederjans will make his professional debut later this week, and he's going in with a whole lot of confidence.

"My game is in the best place it's ever been," he told PGATour.com.

And that will keep his name trending early and often in the future.

TOM WATSON ENJOYING HIS WEEK AT MASTERS, APRIL 5, 2018

AUGUSTA—Tom Watson can't pick a favorite this week.

There are just too many choices.

As the 82nd Masters teed off Thursday, he said he could not remember a time when so many of the world's top players were playing at the top of their game. In fact, it was as if he almost wished he was in a different profession.

"Without a doubt, the lead-up to this has been the most exciting of any Masters I've ever been associated with," Watson said. "It's got to be a journalist's dream. It's like Christmas. There are so many stories to write and so many sidebars. Whatever you write, everybody's going to be interested."

While Watson was unable to settle on one particular favorite, he did iterate that he felt like it was going to be a week for the "old guys."

"I think Tiger (Woods) is going to be right there," Watson said. "I think Phil (Mickelson) will be right there. If there's a dark horse, I like Henrik Stenson. It may be his time."

Watson got the week off on the right start for the "old guys" Wednesday. The 68-year-old two-time Masters champion shot a 6-under par 21 to become the oldest to win the annual Par-3 Contest. He broke the mark of Sam Snead, who was 61 when he won the contest in 1974.

With as well as Watson played, did it make him want to tee it up with the rest of the players Thursday?

"Not at all," he said. "The big course is too big for me anymore. You have to carry the ball at least 280 yards to be successful. These greens aren't designed to be hitting long irons and 3-woods into the par 4s. They are designed for 9-irons."

One place that a 280-yard drive would not be required would be on the first tee at 8:15 a.m., when honorary starters Jack Nicklaus and Gary Player got the tournament started. With Watson's career record at Augusta—two wins (1977 and 1981) and three runner-up finishes (1978, '79, '84)—along with six other major titles and 39 PGA Tour wins to his name, Watson would be an obvious choice as an eventual replacement for Arnold Palmer in the role.

Palmer died in 2016, and this was the second Masters in which the duo of Nicklaus and Player handled the starting duties on their own. But Watson, who considered Palmer his longtime idol, did not want to consider the idea.

"That's not my decision," he said. "(Nicklaus and Player) are in a class above me, and I'm sure they will continue to handle the duties for years to come."

Watson last played the Masters in 2016. Around that same time, he curtailed his schedule to play only seven or eight events on the PGA Tour Champions circuit, and that will be the case again this year. He will play next week in the Mitsubishi Electric Classic in Duluth and, the following week, with partner Andy North at the Legends of Golf in Watson's home state of Missouri.

Watson is also looking forward to playing the senior majors, including the Senior British Open at the home of golf—the Old Course at St. Andrews.

With more time away from the game, Watson is focusing his time on two of his other passions.

First, his wife, Hilary, who was diagnosed with cancer late last year and is currently undergoing chemotherapy treatment.

"So far, so good," Watson said. "She's doing well and the prognosis is good, but we won't know anything for sure until next month."

The other is cutting horse competitions—2 and a half-minute equestrian events where a rider and horse must separate two cows from a herd. Hilary Watson has been competing in these events for almost eight years, and the more Tom watched, the more he wanted to be a part of it.

Watson has been competing in the horse shows for a year-and-a-half and has made more than $7,000 in prize money, but just like in golf, equestrian competitors have their slumps.

Watson said he is in the midst of one.

"I haven't been performing as well as I would like," he said. "I competed in shows in Texas and Oklahoma and (didn't get out of the first round), so I went to a two-day clinic put on by Michael Cooper (a re-nowned cutting horse trainer). I learned how to ride the horse better, and I learned some things."

Watson said there are parallels between cutting and golf. A lot of cutting is done through feel and, he said, the human condition.

"Walking into the pen slowly, I have some nerves," Watson said, "but when the guy gives me the command (to go), the nerves disappear. I'm all in. I'm ready to go."

And as he has always done in golf, Watson is going to continue to practice, improve and be the best he can be. He said there may even be an area where he has an advantage over more experienced riders.

"I think I have a little advantage because I've been in a big arena and dealt with the pressure," Watson said. "It's just who I am. I enjoy playing and taking on the best competition. I enjoy trying to beat people.

"All my life, I've gotten to play a game for a living. I'm a pretty lucky guy."

MASTERS UP FOR YOUNG SPIETH'S TAKING, APRIL 13, 2014

No first-time player has won the Masters since Fuzzy Zoeller did in in 1979.

Today, that drought is going to end --- and it will end thanks to a 20-year old.

But Jordan Spieth is not your typical 20-year-old. He's a young guy with a mature game. He also has enough knowledge to know what he doesn't know, and considering the subtleties of Augusta National Golf Club, that would be a lot, so Spieth found some people with some sage advice.

He started by talking with Carl Jackson, Ben Crenshaw's longtime caddie at Augusta National, who has caddied all 43 Masters that Crenshaw has played in, and a few extra.

Then he sought out Crenshaw himself. The two-time Masters champion loves to teach younger players the finer points of the course. He loves it even more when the players he talks with does what he says.

And finally, Spieth went to Jack Nicklaus, the six-time Masters champion and arguably the greatest player of all time.

Combined, the trio represents more than 130 years of Masters experience.

"I had a talk with Mr. Nicklaus, and he helped me out," Spieth said. "This was Wednesday evening at a dinner here.

"I really don't want to get into specifics about what was said, because I don't…but, yeah, certain things."

Spieth didn't have to say what Nicklaus told him. We already knew, because the Golden Bear let us in on a secret Thursday morning.

He said that a couple of the younger players these days come to ask for his advice, but not many. But when they do, Nicklaus said he is always willing to answer any questions they have.

After that, he asked us a question.

"Why would you ever aim for anything other than the middle of the greens here?" he said.

From there, he pointed out that players who aim for the middle of the greens are likely going to have a good angle to putt from without much of the severity that comes with putting the ball on the wrong side of the hole.

This is what Spieth said after his 2-under par round got him into today's final group with Bubba Watson.

"I've never picked so many targets at the middle of the greens when I see the pins on the side and committed to it.

"I'm like, well, I want to go at the pin, but you can't do that here."

Heading into today's round, Spieth is one of only two players in the field to play under-par golf all-three days, joining fellow first-timer Jonas Blixt. He's shot 71, 70 and 70, and he's only three-putted twice.

When Nicklaus won his 18 majors and 73 PGA Tour titles, he didn't do it by making more birdies than everyone else. He did it by making more pars and letting everyone else around him make the mistakes — i.e. Watson (74 on Saturday), Adam Scott (76) and John Senden (75) who were all in front of Spieth when the day started.

This isn't to say that Spieth is going to be the next Jack Nicklaus, but it looks like he's taken Nicklaus' advice to heart.

"As far as being patient shot-to-shot, I think I've done that the best I've ever had with my mental game," Spieth said. "A lot of it this week has been, 'We're going to be all right. We'll make bogey at worst. Hit the smart shot and you take your birdies where you can get them.' My putter feels great, and that's leading to a lot of confidence in the rest of my game."

If Spieth wins, he will become the youngest Masters champion and one of the youngest to ever win a major title. He will have already earned more than $8 million, been a member of the Presidents Cup team and will have likely wrapped up a spot on this fall's Ryder Cup team.

All that will be left to see is if someone says about Spieth what Arnold Palmer said about Nicklaus after the Golden Bear won his first major at the 1962 U.S. Open.

"Now that the big guy's out of the cage," Palmer said at the time, "everybody better run for cover."

NICKLAUS FINALLY GOT HIS GREEN JACKET, APRIL 13, 2019

Jack Nicklaus has won six green jackets, but it wasn't until he made a run at a seventh that he actually got one of his own.

Every fan of the Masters knows the winner gets a green jacket. They are presented with one in the Butler Cabin, and then again at the actual awards ceremony on Sunday night. But what most don't know is that isn't the winner's actual jacket. It is one of a member, who is similar enough in size.

After all the ceremonies are done, the champion is measured for a new jacket to be made for him. Somehow, that slipped through the cracks when it came to the greatest champion the game has ever seen. He ended up wearing another famous, or infamous, person's jacket for years. It wasn't until after he was honored with a plaque, on a drinking fountain between the 16th and 17th holes, for his career accomplishments, the club realized its mistake.

"When I won, they brought out a jacket," Nicklaus said. "It was a 46-long and I was a 43-regular and it didn't quite fit.

"So the next year when I came back, they didn't ask me to go get a jacket. They didn't do anything, never mentioned my jacket. Tom Dewey had a jacket, the former governor (of New York), who lost to (Harry)Truman for the presidency (Chicago Daily Tribune headline: Dewey defeats Truman). His jacket fit me and I wore his jacket for probably 15 years, maybe longer. Nobody ever mentioned, 'Do you have your green jacket?' Well, I had Tom Dewey's. I never got a green jacket.

"Finally, I won six Masters. Still, nobody had ever given me a green jacket. I always thought that's what we won here at Augusta National, but never did get one. So, I told the story to (former Augusta National chairman) Jack Stephens in 1998 when we were getting ready to do the drinking fountain at 17. Jack Stephens said, 'What? You've never been given a green jacket?'

I said, "No. Nobody's ever mentioned it."

"He said, OK."

Nicklaus, at 58-years-old, would rattle the pines with cheers one more time that week. He shot a final-round 68, and when he made birdie on No. 15, he briefly moved within two shots of the lead. He would end up finishing sixth.

The following spring, the jacket situation was finally resolved. When Nicklaus went to his locker, he found a note from Stephens.

"It read, 'You will go down to the pro shop and you will be fit for your green jacket,' which is the one I've got on," Nicklaus said.

AN UNBELIEVABLE COMEBACK IS COMPLETE, APRIL 14, 2019

When Jack Nicklaus won the 1986 Masters, his victory seemed most improbable.

At 46-years-old, he found a way to beat the likes of Greg Norman, Seve Ballesteros, Tom Watson and Tom Kite—all members of the World Golf Hall of Fame.

It was Nicklaus' 18th professional major victory, and it was the best Masters ever played, until now.

Tiger Woods found another way to eclipse the "Golden Bear," by birdieing three of his last six holes for a one-shot victory on Sunday. The win was his 15th major championship, the first since 2008 and his first Masters since 2005.

It also completed the most unlikely comeback of an athlete to the top of their sport of all time.

When Nicklaus won in '86, he hadn't won a PGA Tour event in two years and had gone six years without winning a major. At 46 it was called a great comeback, and as unlikely as it was, it wasn't a comeback. All the win did was end a bad stretch of golf. He was still ranked No. 33 in the world.

Sunday, Woods beat a field that featured 25 of the top 50 players in the world, all playing at the top of their game.

Plus, he finally overcame the injuries, the four back and four knee surgeries that led to missing large portions of seasons, and the scandals that ended his marriage, and forced him to get help for an addiction to painkillers.

Woods had to deal with all of it, and along the way his game completely crashed and burned. During one comeback attempt, his short game was so bad he had the chipping yips. After spending more than 13 years at No. 1, his world ranking fell to 1,199th.

With his win, Woods is back to No. 6.

This was a comeback.

What he has done the last two years to get back on top isn't just improbable, it's almost impossible to imagine, even for him.

"I had serious doubts after what transpired a couple years ago," he said. "I could barely walk. I couldn't sit. I couldn't lay down. I really couldn't do much of anything.

"Luckily I had the procedure on my back, which gave me a chance at having a normal life. But then all of a sudden, I realized I could actually swing a golf club again. I was very fortunate to be given another chance to do something that I love to do."

With that realization, we now see a more grateful, more accessible, a more likable Tiger Woods. Now, he's not afraid to smile, give someone a high-five and have a little fun with his playing partners.

He also has come to the realization that he can do those things, and then go out and play championship golf. On Sunday, he played better and thought his way around the course better than anybody else.

While Francesco Molinari and Tony Finau found ways to make putts and stay at the top on the front nine, Woods remained patient. Once the players moved to the back nine, he allowed Molinari, Finau, Brooks Koepka and the others to make the mistakes.

Woods hit it in the middle of the green on 12, Molinari, Finau and Koepka all hit it in the water.

On 15, Woods hit it in the middle of the green in two. Xander Schauffele hit his drive in the trees, had to lay up, and then hit his wedge over the green.

On 16, Koepka and Patrick Cantlay hit tee shots too far right and left themselves with near impossible downhill putts. Woods hit his tee shot in the middle of the green and let the ball follow the slope and down to the hole—just over one foot from the hole.

That birdie gave Woods a two-shot lead and the cushion he needed to finish off the victory, and brought out roars that hadn't reverberated through Augusta National since Nicklaus in '86.

It was the kind of play that inspired the current generation of players. The guys like Koepka, Justin Thomas, Rickie Fowler and others to not only take up the game, but play like him—hit it long, make every putt and win.

For most of their careers, they could only see Woods' best golf on YouTube videos. They always said they wanted to know what it was like to play against Woods in his prime. They got a glimpse of what he could do in last year's British Open and PGA. At the Tour Championship at East Lake, Woods finally broke through with a victory, and the younger players found out how Woods moves the needle.

Sunday, they found out Woods' "prime" may not quite be complete. They loved it, and they know the comeback is complete.

"You just look at the last five years and what he's had to go through," Koepka said. "I mean, to come back, get back playing and back to where he was, get his body back in shape. To be able to come back out here and have the Tiger of old—as a fan, I love it. I think it's awesome. I'm glad he's back. It's probably one of the coolest things to be a part of it, even though you finished second place, you know, you're a little bummed out.

"You know, you want to play against the best to ever play. You want to go toe-to-toe with them, and you know, I can leave saying I gave it my all. He's just good, man."

When Woods reached the clubhouse, a large group of those players he inspired were there to greet him—Schauffele, Koepka, Fowler and Thomas were lined up with Bubba Watson, Ian Poulter, Zach Johnson and Bernhard Langer. They all shared handshakes and hugs.

Nicklaus too, sent congratulations.

"A big 'Well done,' from me to Tiger," he said on social media. "I am so happy for him and the game of golf. This is just fantastic."

It's been a long road back for Woods. At 43, he's finally here.

Hopefully he can stay awhile and give us a few more moments like the 2019 Masters to remember.

HIGH SCHOOL FOOTBALL

BRADLEY CHUBB RETURNS TO HILLGROVE TO SPEAK TO PRESENT-DAY HAWKS, NOVEMBER 9, 2018

POWDER SPRINGS — As a freshman at North Carolina State, Bradley Chubb wanted to transfer.

He arrived in Raleigh as one the Wolfpack's top recruits, but he was relegated to fourth string on the depth chart and limited to playing special teams.

Chubb was unhappy, felt the team was unhappy and he felt a new location would do him good.

Then, he looked in the mirror.

"I realized it was me," Chubb said Friday as he addressed the football team and other students at Hillgrove High School, his alma mater. "I was feeling sorry for myself, wasn't putting out my best effort, wasn't eating right and I wasn't studying my playbook."

After a conversation with his parents, Chubb returned to N.C. State with a better frame of mind and went to work. Over the following years, he continued to improve and, when he left the Wolfpack after the 2017 season, he had recorded 25 sacks and 54 and a half tackles for loss.

Chubb left college as a first-team All-American and the Atlantic Coast Conference Defensive Player of the Year. He also won the Ted

Hendricks Award as the nation's best defensive lineman and the Bronco Nagurski Award as the nation's best defensive player.

Less than 24 hours before speaking at Hillgrove, Chubb was honored at N.C. State by having his No. 9 jersey retired and hung in Carter-Finley Stadium.

On Friday, however, he was back where it all started as he talked to students about hard work, perseverance and reaching for their goals.

"If you are in a bad situation and there's things in your way, don't complain," Chubb said. "Everything you want in life, you have to go get. You can't wait around for someone to hand it to you, because that isn't going to happen."

While he was at the school, Chubb presented Hillgrove coach Phillip Ironside a game-used No. 55 jersey from the Denver Broncos, who took Chubb with the fourth overall pick of last April's NFL draft.

Chubb is the fourth Hillgrove alum currently on an NFL roster, joining the Miami Dolphins' Kenyan Drake, the New York Giants' Evan Engram and Chubb's brother, Brandon, who is currently on the Carolina Panthers' practice squad.

Bradley Chubb also explained Friday that high school is not too early to have a career-changing moment.

As a junior at Hillgrove, he tore his ACL and missed the majority of the season. At the time, he was just starting to get recruited, and he said he probably was not the best defensive lineman on the team.

It was another conversation with his parents that brought him around.

"I had my head down," Chubb said. "I didn't know if football was for me."

Football was definitely for him.

After being drafted by the Broncos, it allowed Chubb the opportunity to learn from the player he emulated, All-Pro outside linebacker Von Miller.

As happy as Chubb was to play with Miller, the veteran was equally as excited to play with the rookie. Miller posted a video online of his reaction when the team drafted, jumping up and down and screaming with delight.

It was a compliment Chubb said that he will always remember.

"It meant the world to me," he said, "to see how much he wanted me there meant a lot."

Chubb said Miller has taken him under his wing and now, nine games into the season, Chubb's play has taken off. He has 30 tackles, a forced fumble and is sixth in the NFL with eight sacks.

It leaves him on pace to earn the things he set as goals for his rookie season.

"I want to be Defensive Rookie of the Year," Chubb said, "and the rookie sack record is 14 and a half. I'd love to get that. But, most importantly, I want to win games on the NFL level."

The Broncos are on their bye week this week, which allowed Chubb to attend his jersey retirement at N.C. State and speak at Hillgrove. He also said he would be on the sideline Friday night to watch the Hawks take on Pebblebrook in the opening round of the Class AAAAAAA playoffs, and he said he would be the one cheering the loudest.

Most importantly, though, Chubb said it was just good being home.

"It feels amazing," he said about coming back to Hillgrove. "When you're in school, you dream about stuff like this. It's great to be able to come back to talk to the kids."

FAMILY AFFAIR: KELL'S TIGHT-KNIT SECONDARY MAY BE THE BEST IN GEORGIA HIGH SCHOOL FOOTBALL, AUGUST 19, 2012

Kell defensive back Taylor Henkle is in a unique situation.

A junior entering his third year as a starter in the Longhorns secondary, he has grown into a quiet leader of a unit that already features two seniors who are going to be playing on Saturday—Brendan Langley, who recently committed to South Carolina, and Quincy Mauger, who will be heading to Georgia.

It can make for an interesting dynamic, considering the player with the most experience is younger than the higher profile recruits, but according to Kell coach Derek Cook, there is a reason that the rest of the unit shows him that kind of respect.

"Henkle has lost four games total since the fifth grade," Kell coach Derek Cook said. "He almost wills things to happen. He just refuses to lose."

The 5-foot-10, 180-pound Henkle learned some of that quality from having a chance to play alongside Brian Randolph, the former Kell star and a freshman all-American at safety for the University of Tennessee. Cook said Henkle soaked in the advice Randolph provided and watched his work ethic and approach to playing the game. The mentorship rubbed off on Henkle, who is also getting Division I interest from Georgia Tech, Clemson, Oregon and Florida. He became a pillar in a unit that has taken on a family dynamic, and that family may be the best defensive backfield in Georgia high school football. It's already one that produced nearly 400 tackles and 16 interceptions in 2011.

"We have different types of guys with different personalities," Henkle said. "I keep my calm and focus. Langley and (Jay) Moxey keep guys pumped up. Quincy is a passionate type of leader and then there's Julian (Burris)."

Burris is the one guy that isn't an official starter, but he may see the most field time of all of them in the defensive backfield. He is the family's "Jack-of-all-trades", and he is a nice "Jack" to have, considering the junior is 5-10, 170 pounds and runs a 4.4 second 40-yard dash. Regardless of which of the other four rotate off the field, Burris has the ability to take their spot and there is no drop in level of play.

"He has a feel for the game other people don't have," Cook said. "All I know is he seems to be in the right place to make plays a lot."

As future SEC players, it could be easy for Langley and Mauger to carry an elitist type of air, and boast about the accomplishments they have already achieved, but they know that is no way to influence the up-and-coming players on the Longhorns squad, and Cook said it is important that they understand that responsibility.

"Kids follow the high impact players most of the time," he said. "And 99 percent of the time I'm pleased with what they bring to the table."

Langley is the outgoing, gregarious member of the group. He can often be seen laughing and playing around with friends and teammates, but when it's time to play, he's nothing but serious. At 6-1, 187-pounds. with a 4.4 40, Langley is one that can get inside an opponents' head. He knows he's good, the opponent knows he's good, and he knows the opponent knows he's good. And it all came full circle in less than a year.

"As a sophomore I didn't even play defense," said Langley, who finished his first season at cornerback with 59 tackles and six interceptions.

Despite the newness to the position, Langley impressed enough college scouts to land 14 offers from Bowl Championship Subdivision schools, including 11 from the SEC. Langley said much of his success stems from the unit working so well together.

"It's our ability to function and cooperate," he said. "We trust each other on and off the field and it allows us to take risks during the game because if we make a mistake, someone will be able to make up for it."

Langley added that as he became an upperclassman, things became clearer and he took the game more seriously. Like the rest of the unit, that maturity goes a long way.

"We have a chance to make this defense the best in Kell history," he said. "These guys are phenomenal athletes and we play wise beyond our years."

The 6-foot, 197 pound Mauger, who finished the 2011 season with 102 tackles, agrees.

"We are very well disciplined and we know our keys," he said. "But more importantly, we make sure everyone has fun."

The final member of the family is everyone's little brother in Moxey. He is only 5-5 and 152 pounds, but this will be his second year as a starter. And while his stature may be small, his game is big, finishing last season with four interceptions.

Moxey said he still has a growth spurt in him, but he summed up perfectly what the Kell defensive backs believe in, and what will make them a solid team again in 2012.

"We do what we have to do."

MASON'S BELIEFS TAKE HIM FURTHER THAN THE FOOTBALL FIELD, OCTOBER 23, 2009

Hutson Mason is a patient man of faith.

In today's world of instant gratification and the every-thing-has-to-be-done-yesterday mentality, it's not the normal trait you would expect to find in an 18-year-old, let alone Lassiter High School's most recognizable athlete.

Mason's patience is an invaluable asset when he takes the field at quarterback.

So far this season, he has led the Trojans to a 7-0 record, thrown for 2,377 yards and connected with his receivers for 26 touchdowns. Mason has completed 76 percent of his passes, thrown only three interceptions in 209 attempts and, last week, his 545 passing yards set a new Georgia high school state record.

But for all his patience letting him be successful on the field, it is

Mason's faith off the field that is most impressive, and something he is leaning on as he juggles football, his academics, his rightful change from being a teenager into a man and what is becoming a more stressful and mind-boggling recruiting process.

"My faith is a huge part of who I am," he said.

Mason comes from a very religious family. He is a member of the First Baptist Church in Woodstock and offers his teammates and other friends and classmates from Lassiter a chance to meet with him and others in a weekly bible study, as he did Tuesday night.

In those meetings, Mason said it is an opportunity for fellowship, a chance to talk about personal issues and a chance to listen and learn from an occasional guest speaker. But on Tuesday, it was Mason who did the talking, and he talked about his patience and how he is able to stay calm when a big decision on his future and where he will go to college will soon need to be made.

"(The recruiting process) was one of the big reasons I talked about that (Tuesday)," he said.

For good reason.

For someone with such gaudy numbers—who threw for 3,705 yards as a junior, was Class AAAAA's Offensive Player of the Year and is a mere four months from National Signing Day—Mason has offers from only four Football Bowl Subdivision schools: Eastern Michigan, Western Michigan, UAB and Indiana, none of which ring through with any big-time football tradition.

Originally, Iowa offered Mason a scholarship, which he came very close to accepting, but the Hawkeyes got an in-state quarterback to commit and pulled Mason's offer from the table just before he made the decision.

Despite the disappointment, just like he stands in the huddle, Mason remains cool and calm.

But it begs the question.

Why are the scholarship offers so slow to present themselves?

To this point, no college coach has told him of any significant drawbacks in his game.

Lassiter coach Chip Lindsey said it's not that bigger schools aren't looking at Mason, it's just that he is consistently the third or fourth quarterback on their recruiting board.

Is it his size?

Not at a solid 6-foot-3.

Is it a lack of arm strength?

While it's true in looking at many of the Lassiter games on DVD, Mason cannot be found throwing a deep out. But, any question of arm strength should have been answered last week against Milton. While rolling left, Mason squared his hips and shoulders and threw a pass across his body 50 yards down the middle of the field for a long gain.

Eliminating size and arm strength, it leaves other facts. One, Mason is never under center. He takes every snap from the shotgun, and no one is going to mistake him for Usain Bolt anytime soon. It seems as if many college coaches see Mason as nothing more than a system quarterback.

But even to those coaches, 545 yards passing is hard to ignore, and it may have opened a few others eyes.

Since Saturday, Mason said he has heard from coaches at Mississippi State, Arkansas, Georgia Tech and Tennessee. And, truth be told, in a perfect world Mason would like to wear orange, run through the "T" and out onto Neyland Stadium as a Volunteer.

"If I could go anywhere, it would be to Tennessee," he said. "My uncle went there, my old quarterback coach (Tee Martin) went there, and that's where I'd want to go. Saturday, when they called again, they invited me up for another visit and said they would like to sit down and talk 1-on-1."

Mason's favorite piece of scripture from the Bible comes from Mark 11:24 and reads:

"Therefore I say unto you, what thing so ever ye desire, when ye pray, believe that ye receive them, and ye shall have them."

Or, in layman's terms, as it says on Mason's Facebook page: "So, I tell you to believe that you have received the things you ask for in prayer, and God will give them to you."

It sounds like the old adage may be true—"Patience is a virtue"—and for Mason, at least until he signs his name on a National Letter of Intent in February, he's just going to keep on keeping the faith.

THE ULTIMATE WARRIOR FRED KEY A FIXTURE AT NORTH COBB GAMES, OCTOBER 27, 2008

If it's a Friday night during the high school football season, you can expect to find Acworth resident Fred Key in the stands watching his beloved North Cobb Warriors.

How can you recognize him? He's the one with the letter jacket that reads: Fred, 401 consecutive games. That's right, the 80-year-old Key has been to every game, home and away, regular season or postseason, rain or shine since the beginning of the 1970 season.

"It's been really fun," Key said. It's been really exciting for me."

For Key's dedication to the North Cobb program, he was recognized at halftime of the Warriors game against Marietta last Friday. The team went as far as to slightly alter the traditional yard markings on the field, where instead of the traditional 40, the yard lines read 401 and were outlined in Key's favorite color—North Cobb orange.

"He's our biggest fan," said North Cobb coach Shane Queen. "Anybody that has that kind of passion, you have to listen to his story."

Key's story—at least where North Cobb is involved—began in 1963 when he, his wife, Ruth, and three young sons moved into the Warriors' school district. Knowing his sons would eventually attend the school; Key and his wife adopted North Cobb as their own.

His sons—Jerry, Larry and Tony—all played football for North Cobb and all earned scholarships to play football at Delta State in Mississippi. And that's why his consecutive game streak is 401 and not 471.

"I've only missed three games since 1963," said Key, who missed those games in 1969 to go watch his oldest son, Jerry, play his college games. "My wife and I used to leave on Friday night to drive to Mississippi. But after three times I looked at her and said we could comfortably make the (eight-hour) drive on Saturday because the games were played in the evening. I told her lets stay home on Friday and go watch North Cobb."

His youngest son, Tony, graduated in 1976, but Key continued to work on the chain crew until 1980 when he said Ruth asked him, "Don't you think it's time you came up here in the stands and watch the games with me."

Key relented to her request, but remained involved with the team by going to the school, loading the team's equipment in the back of his 1977 Ford pickup truck for road games and transporting it to wherever the Warriors might be playing. To this day, Key still transports equipment to the road games, and he still does it in the same 1977 pickup. When asked how many miles he has on the truck, Key said, "I don't know, but the truck is on its third motor. Whenever one quits I put a new one in it."

Key said Ruth loved football as much as he did, unfortunately she stopped watching the games with him in 2002 when she passed away ending another impressive streak—one of 53 years and four months of marriage.

"God, I still miss that woman," he said.

Since her passing, Key continues to work. He's sold pine straw since 1989.

"I enjoy working and meeting people," he said.

He also has a few other hobbies to keep him busy. Key owns a houseboat on one of the area lakes where he can often be seen fishing with Dammit, his Jack Russell Terrier.

He also enjoys disco dancing. Most Saturday nights Key can be found boogieing on the dance floors of some of the local clubs on Sandy Plains Road, and he continues to have a soft spot for persons of the female persuasion.

"I'm looking for a girlfriend," Key said, but he added there are two prerequisites any potential companion must meet. "She has to dance and she has to like sports."

However, no matter how many hobbies he has, nothing occupies Key's time like North Cobb football.

During the season, he can be seen strolling through the weight room at the high school talking with the players, offering to take them fishing and just having a good time.

"I love being around the kids that are high school aged," Key said. "They keep me young."

He said he has always joked that if he was in the hospital on a Friday night before a North Cobb game, somebody had better come and get him or he would hitchhike to the stadium.

Many people don't know, last year he proved it.

With about three week's left in the Warriors' run to an undefeated 2007 regular season, Key was walking in his driveway when he said he was stricken with "the worst pain I've ever had in my life."

A pain so intense in his leg it literally knocked him off his feet and on to his hands and knees, leaving him needing help to get back to the house. When his son, Jerry, came over to check on him, Key's son said, "Well, I guess you won't be going to the North Cobb game on Friday."

"I said, you wanna bet," Key said.

Originally thought to be a sciatic nerve problem, Key got some crutches and went to the game. When it became too hard to maneuver, two of his sons carried him into the stadium and his grandson carried him out piggyback style.

The following Monday, when he finally went to the doctor, he ended up in the emergency room. Key had a clogged artery in his right leg and had to undergo an angioplasty—a procedure where a balloon is passed through the artery to clear the blockage. He had the procedure early in the week, and was at the Warriors' game that Friday.

Key said he will attend North Cobb football games as long has he is healthy enough to do so. And anyone who wants to know how many games the streak is at, all they have to do is look at Key's letter jacket.

The jacket was presented to him for his 50th wedding anniversary by former coach Bob Clark and each week Key updates his scoreboard by hand sewing the new number in place. And, if anyone sees Key this Friday when the Warriors travel to Etowah, that number will read 402.

A SMILE, A 'MAGICAL YOUNG MAN,' IS GONE, FEBRUARY 19, 2010

A contagious smile, a firm handshake and a confident, "Yes, sir."

That was the last thing Rajaan Bennett said to me after I wished him good luck on National Signing Day earlier this month. It came right after I had the pleasure of standing next to him for a group picture with most of the area's top signees.

Now, I could have stood next to any one of the guys who signed that day, but Rajaan had that air of success that drew people to him. It was a quiet confidence that was going to serve him well at Vanderbilt, and as a man once he got out of college.

All that was true.

Until early Thursday.

In the wee hours of the morning, the ex-boyfriend of Rajaan's mother came to their house. There, Clifton Steger shot Rajaan and his uncle before turning the gun on himself.

Rajaan and Steger were pronounced dead at the scene.

What a waste.

Gone in an instant were not just the hopes and dreams of an 18-year-old football star, but a son, a role model and a friend who the majority of the McEachern and Cobb football communities admired and respected.

The loss of Rajaan hit members of the football team so hard that it was too difficult for them to put their feelings in words. McEachern athletic director Jimmy Dorsey tried to say it for them.

"He was a magical young man," said Dorsey, who was Rajaan's coach his first two seasons in high school. "He was one of a kind. He was the complete package.

"This is something that happens to people that put themselves in a bad situation. This is so unfair, because Rajaan did everything right."

At 5-foot-10 and 210 pounds, Rajaan was built to carry a football. He had just completed a senior season in which he rushed for more than 1,850 yards and scored 28 touchdowns. He had Barry Sanders-esque moves where he could start, stop or shift directions in a split second, and while he may not have had the greatest speed, no one ever seemed to be able to catch him in the open field.

Rajaan was named all-region, all-county and all-state. He was the Class AAAAA Offensive Player of the Year and, with a stroke of a pen, became one of the biggest recruiting steals Vanderbilt has pulled off in the last decade. His potential was endless. An NFL career was a real possibility.

What a waste.

Gone in an instant was a true student-athlete—a young man who was going to graduate from McEachern in May with a 3.8 grade-point average with an eye on being an architect. He was intelligent, and it wasn't just book smarts. Life had already passed on an education from the school of hard knocks.

The man of the house since losing his father six years ago, Rajaan graciously took on the role of caretaker of his younger sister and special-needs brother when his mother could not be home. He took the matter so seriously that, when schedules conflicted, he left his role as a part of the Indians' basketball team to make sure they were properly cared for.

And he did it all with the same contagious smile on his face. Every time I saw him, whether we were keeping him on the field too long during a photo shoot, or boring him with some of my questions, he always had that smile.

Rajaan was on his way. He was excited to be heading to Vanderbilt. He was excited to be reaching his goals and he was already making a mark on his future teammates.

"I spent a lot of time with him and got to know him real well," said Walton defensive end and Vanderbilt signee Kyle Woestmann. "I was excited to know I was going to be going with him (to Vanderbilt), and I knew I'd have the chance to be with him four or five years, tackling him every day on the practice field.

"When coach (Rocky) Hidalgo called me (to tell me what happened), it broke my heart. It's amazing how some of the best people in the world get dealt the worst. It's a waste of possibly the best person I've met in my life. The fact that somebody made that big of an impression (on me, so fast), speaks for itself."

I couldn't have said it any better.

I just wish the folks at Vanderbilt could see what we had the honor to see the last few years.

What a talent. What a student. What a man.

Gone in an instant.

What a waste.

RAJAAN DESERVED ANOTHER TYPE OF SATURDAY CROWD, SEPTEMBER 11, 2011

POWDER SPRINGS—It was a perfect morning leading to what would've been a perfect day of college football.

There was a coolness in the air as the sun was trying to break through the clouds. Music was playing as the crowd began to gather. People were talking, laughing and the smell of food on the grill floated on the breeze.

Everyone stood at attention for the national anthem, and, afterward, there was loud applause.

It was a scene Rajaan Bennett was supposed to be experiencing as a Vanderbilt running back Saturday in Nashville, Tenn., as the Commodores were preparing to take on Ole Miss in their Southeastern Conference opener.

Only, there was no kickoff. There was a crowd of about 80 instead of 80,000. And, instead of a football game, close friends and relatives came to see the Powder Springs Community Task Force honor Rajaan by dedicating a bench in his memory near the fountain in Powder Springs' town square.

Task Force chairman Jerry Houston said the choice of the wrought-iron bench could be seen as a symbolic one.

"It's meant to be seen as a sign of stability and strength," he said. "We wanted to do something because of the importance that he had in our lives."

As a senior at McEachern in 2009, Bennett rushed for more than 1,850 yards, 28 touchdowns and was named the Associated Press Class AAAAA Offensive Player of the Year. His efforts on the football field garnered a scholarship to showcase his skills in the SEC, and he was well on his way to a potential NFL career.

It's been nearly two years since that tragic February day, when Bennett was gunned down in his own home by an intruder who was once considered a family friend. But it's not the football Rajaan's family and friends remember, it's the man he was becoming, the life that he lived and the effect he still has on people.

"It's a daily thing," McEachern girls basketball coach Phyllis Arthur said. "Every day, athletes and non-athletes talk about him and about how much they miss him.

"He comes up every day, because I use him as an example. All the time, I tell kids to carry yourself like Rajaan did."

While football was always an important part of Rajaan's life, what still stands out to those who knew him was that, regardless of how dominant a player he could be, sports were never his top priority.

God was first, family came second. Rajaan was the man of the house at age 10 after his father died in a car accident, and he took on the responsibility of taking care of his mother, Narjaketha, and his two younger siblings.

His school work came third, and he proved it by carrying a 3.8 grade-point average with the hopes of becoming an architect.

"Rajaan was the one that taught us it was cool to get good grades," said former classmate Janine Laura. "And it was the blueprint he left behind how he showed us how to live life."

Finally, there was time for Rajaan to be Rajaan, which meant out-working everyone on the football field, in the weight room and in the film room.

And, not to be forgotten, he always found a little time to have some fun and flash that big, beaming smile.

"From a team perspective, he was the guy everybody was inspired to be," said Andrew Guerrier, the student pastor at Trinity Chapel in

Powder Springs and a 5-year representative of Fellowship of Christian Athletes. "He was the guy everyone was inspired to be like."

That wasn't just in the locker room at McEachern.

"All over the county, everyone knew Rajaan was a force to be reckoned with," Guerrier said, "and they all respected him. But it's hard to understand what kind of a person he was if you didn't get to know him. Once he was gone, and the stories came out about him, a lot of athletes began to understand what he was all about.

"And a lot of athletes have been influenced by his adoption of scripture."

When the memorial was unveiled, Narjaketha Bennett was given the chance to speak. Long pauses came between the few words she offered, but what she said rang true.

"Everything seems like it was just yesterday," she said, "but I know he's still with me."

In the end, Rajaan led his life strongly and influenced anyone who wanted to take the time to learn from it. Houston said that's one of the reasons the memorial bench was placed where it is.

It faces east.

"The sun rises in the east," Houston said. "Now, when the sun rises, so will the spirit of Rajaan Bennett."

CAROLE KELL LIKE A PROUD MOTHER WATCHING 'HORNS WIN, AUGUST 25, 2010

The happiest person on the sidelines Saturday afternoon as Kell put the finishing touches on a 13-10 victory over Grayson in the Corky Kell Classic wasn't head coach Derek Cook.

It wasn't athletic director Peter Giles or principal Trudie Donovan, nor was it any of the approximately 70 football players.

No, the happiest person in the Georgia Dome that day was Carole Kell, the wife of the Classic's creator and namesake.

"I was excited as I've ever been," Carole said. "It was about finally getting there, playing in it and winning."

For the Longhorns to play in the Corky Kell Classic, it was the completion of a journey that started years before under Carole's careful watch, with the full intention of having a school named after her husband, Corky, the former Wheeler football coach and longtime Cobb County athletic director.

After working 33 years in the Cobb County school system, and 14 years as a principal at either Dickerson or Hightower Trail middle schools, Carole knew how the system worked. In order to have a building named for someone, the honoree must be dead for at least three years, and then letters are written to the school board on the honoree's behalf.

Carole had little trouble getting people to write letters for Corky.

"They came from everywhere," she said, "because people appreciated him. There was a huge stack of letters because he knew everybody in the state.

"And people appreciated him. They all wrote about the experiences they had with Corky, and they all knew his goal. No matter what it was, his goal was to do right by the children."

It appeared as if her quest was about to end when the system was building a school back in the late '90 just west of Cobb Parkway. That school would instead become Kennesaw Mountain.

It wasn't until the fall of 2002, when Carlton J. Kell High School opened its doors, that Carole's efforts finally paid off. At the time, she didn't know where the next school would be built in the county, but it was a happy coincidence when she found out it was going to be built in the neighborhood she lives in. And from the time the first shovel hit the ground, Carole knew she had to try and get the Longhorns into the Corky Kell Classic.

The effort gained full steam when Cook became the Longhorns' coach three years ago.

"Every year, (Cook) takes me to lunch to give me the report on how the team is going to play," Carole said. "And every year, we've plotted on how we can get Kell into the Classic."

Of course, the politicking didn't end there. Dave Hunter, the former coach of Brookwood High School and now executive director of the Classic, would playfully try to avoid Carole each time he saw her, because he knew he was about to get an earful. Carole said each time she saw Hunter he would say, "You aren't going to talk to me about Kell (getting in the Classic) again, are you?"

The answer was always yes, but in the end, all it took was some success and back-to-back Class AAAAA playoff appearances.

But getting Kell High School to the Georgia Dome proved to be the easy part. Watching the Longhorns play there proved to be harder than Carole ever imagined.

"When Corky was coaching, I always told him I would never pray for him to win a ballgame," Carole said. "But I said I am going to pray for this one."

With the game tied 3-3 at the half, it didn't take long for Carole's prayer to be answered. In the third quarter, a Taylor Henkle interception set up Kyle Morris' second field goal, and Brian Randolph scored a touchdown a few minutes later to give the Longhorns a relatively comfortable 13-3 lead—relatively comfortable for everyone except Carole, who was trying to watch the game with her grandchildren.

"It got to a point where I didn't even know they were there," she said. "My hands were clenched so hard my muscles hurt the next day."

And as the final seconds ticked off the clock, Carole had a feeling she knew someone, somewhere may have been pulling a few strings.

"I really don't know a word to describe what I was feeling," she said. "But I was convinced Corky's little spirit was around."

Whether he was present at the Dome or not, the hundreds of players who came to play, and the thousands of fans who came to watch, helped continue the legacy of Corky Kell.

"Corky's purpose was to get every kid on the (Georgia Dome) field." Carole said. "To see everyone there, (and to know why he developed the Classic) he has accomplished what he wanted to do."

KOESTER DESERVES CHANCE TO COACH, MAY 17, 2013

Ed Koester wants to coach football.

To the people who know him well, this is no shock. It's something Koester has done in some fashion every day for much of the last 35-plus years, but that changed earlier this year.

In January, after leading South Cobb to a 22-11 record in one of the best three-year stretches of the program's history—which included its first state playoff victory—Koester resigned his position as the Eagles' coach.

At the time, he said the 90-minute commute each day from his home in Cherokee County had become too much, and he wanted to spend more quality time with his family.

While the 57-year-old Koester stands by his statement, others with knowledge of the South Cobb program have suggested otherwise.

They feel the owner of 139 career victories, 16 winning seasons, 13 playoff appearances and five district or region championships as a coach at South Cobb, Cherokee, Arlington Heights in Fort Worth, Texas, and Bixby High School in Oklahoma was pushed off the sideline because he wanted to apply for another job in Cobb County.

When asked to clarify the situation, South Cobb principal Ashley Hosey said he was not allowed to comment on personnel matters, but the irony is, now that Koester has the opportunity to freely search for a new coaching position, he can't find one—not even as an assistant.

But this is not meant to give the impression that Koester is sitting next to a football field waiting for practice to start with a sign that says, "Will coach for food." Because he's not.

Koester is still a teacher at South Cobb. Last year, he earned his doctorate in education, and with his experience in the classroom, he should not have a problem putting food on the table for his family.

But he's missing the big piece that makes him the man he is today—his ability to teach on the field.

So far this spring, Koester says he's applied for at least five head-coaching positions in and around the metro-Atlanta area. In at least two cases, he was led to believe the job was his only to later receive a call to say that particular school would hire from within.

Koester even took a flyer on the job at Savannah State University. With his application, he included letters of recommendation from other coaches he has had the opportunity to work with, including Pope's Matt Kemper.

Kemper's statements were a good indication of what the majority of coaches in Cobb County said about Koester.

"I have been blessed to have coached, or currently coach, three of my own sons," Kemper wrote in his letter. "I would want them on Coach Koester's team. He is the kind of man that is all too rare in coaching today and the kind of man that should be leading a football program and its young men."

Based on the feelings of the coaches in the county, it would seem like a natural fit for Koester to work on one of their staffs next season. The problem is, with the Cobb County School District potentially cutting nearly 200 teaching positions from next year's budget, it's unlikely that there will be a physical education or social studies opening—Koester's areas of teaching expertise—for him to fill. If there are available slots, there's a good chance there would be a recruiting battle for his services.

Unfortunately, one of the other reasons that may be holding Koester back is his age.

He knows that 57 can be a tough hurdle to overcome, but he's proven he can adjust as times change. Koester allowed his players to design South Cobb's new red-fade-to-blue helmet scheme last season, and he has a Twitter account.

But, more importantly, he knows how to win football games.

And there should be no question of his dedication level. Last season, in the week after he helped lead South Cobb to the 300th win in its program's history, he told the story about how he almost made the ultimate sacrifice for his profession.

In 2007, Koester was an assistant on then-coach Derek Cook's South Cobb staff, and the coaches decided it would be a good idea to ride bicycles to practice in order to get there before the players.

This seemed like a good idea until Koester, on a ride to practice, misjudged a ditch. When the bike hit the edge, he flew over the handle bars and quickly found himself lying in the bottom of the trench for 30 minutes without the ability to move.

Initially, some of the coaches and players thought he was kidding around. What had actually happened is Koester had fractured the sixth and seventh lumbar vertebra at the base of his neck. And because of the way he was lying on the ground, the pressure of the injury was not allowing Koester to breathe properly.

All football coaches know, the last thing you do when a player has a neck injury is move him. In Koester's case, he convinced the coaches to go against their better judgment.

"Just before the ambulance got there, on my last breath, I asked them to roll me just a little bit," Koester said. "When they did, it took the pressure off a nerve and my diaphragm kick-started my breathing again. I was about to pass out and I might have died."

Things didn't get much better once he got to the hospital. Twice, he was dropped off an examining table, and doctors mistakenly sent him home without treatment, only to call and have him rush back to the hospital.

And then, when Koester returned, they drilled holes in his skull.

Doctors inserted bolts on either side of Koester's head — similar to the ones sported by the old TV Frankenstein, Herman Munster — to create a makeshift halo device to aid with putting him in traction. For 56 hours, he laid in bed with a 20-pound weight dangling from the device to help take pressure off the damaged vertebrae.

Two weeks later, Koester was back on the field coaching the South Cobb offensive line.

Now, he doesn't know what the future will bring.

Some may see this as bad luck. Others may see it as karma.

All I know is, the job he did at South Cobb with limited resources — no more than five assistant coaches on staff at any time, limited financial help from the booster club and the beginnings of a transient student population — was nothing short of incredible.

If I was hiring a coach, I know who would be at the top of my list.

THE BEST HIGH SCHOOL FOOTBALL PLAYER IN GEORGIA: KELL'S BRIAN RANDOLPH SHOWS HE'S A 60-MINUTE MAN WITH EYES ON TENNESSEE, AUGUST 22, 2010

Ask Kell safety Brian Randolph a question and, in most cases, you are lucky if he answers in more than a few words.

Randolph is quiet, he is reserved and he is shy when it comes to dealing with people outside his inner circle. He said he gets those traits from his father and grandfather. Randolph's mother agrees with the assessment.

"He's a humble person," Lisa Randolph said. "He's not a boaster, but he's not an introvert. He's just quick to the point. Ask him a question and he'll tell you what you want to know."

Put Randolph in a comfortable situation, like on a football field, and things change. The mild-mannered safety and running back becomes aggressive, flies to the football and is willing to put a big hit on a running back or receiver or deliver an equally crushing blow if a defender is standing in his way of the end zone. On the field he shows why he is already a two-time Class AAAAA all-state defensive back and why heading into his senior year may be the best high school player in the state of Georgia.

The attitude that allows Randolph to do all the things he does on the field also comes from his father, Mark, who gave him some words to live by at a young age.

"The biggest advice my dad gave me was 'Big-time players show up in big-time situations.'"

Randolph's ability for the big play was something Kell coach Derek Cook had to learn about his young player when he first accepted the head coaching job at the school three years ago.

Coaches that had been around Randolph came to Cook and said, "This kid is going to be good."

That wasn't the first impression Cook necessarily received from the then-sophomore Randolph.

"When I got here, the coaches kept telling me he was going to be special," Cook said. "But I hadn't seen anything on video that jumped out at me. But then, he hadn't played any defense on film yet."

That all changed in one game against Lassiter.

Randolph hadn't shown much the first two games of the season after becoming the starting free safety, but he used the game against the Trojans as his personal coming out party. He started on offense, rushing for 123 yards and two touchdowns. In the fourth quarter, with Lassiter driving for a potential game-winning touchdown, Randolph stepped in front of a Hutson Mason pass and returned it 90 yards down the sideline to put the game out of reach.

But the biggest thing he did that night was put fear in the hearts of all receivers coming over the middle.

Mason rolled right and threw a short pass to Xavier Morgan, and just as he caught the ball, his momentum came to a screeching halt. Randolph drove through him, lifting Morgan off the ground and depositing him on his back—without the football.

The hit was a crushing blow. It was the kind of hit that shows up on "SportsCenter". The kind of hit that gets a college recruiter's attention—as well as his coach's.

"I went back and watched the tape on that game and he was everywhere," Cook said. "It's one of those games where you watch the tape and just say, 'Whoa.'"

Randolph would finish the 2008 season with 117 tackles and three interceptions. But he also ended the year with an injury.

Randolph originally felt discomfort in his shoulder after playing Woodstock in the 2008 season opener. At the time, he thought it was a stinger with his shoulder going numb. The week after the Lassiter game, something happened again. While trying to make a tackle, his momentum was going one way and he tried to make an arm tackle in the opposite direction. It was the first time his shoulder slid out of place but then popped back in.

"It's hard to describe what I felt," Randolph said. "All I know is it was awful pain."

The injury was diagnosed as a bad bruise that would heal with time. It wasn't until Randolph started playing his junior year he found out the original diagnosis was wrong.

What Randolph had was a torn labrum, the cartilage that keeps the shoulder stable, allowing for a free range of motion. An injury to the labrum he would learn, would also lead to shoulder dislocations, some-thing he suffered more than a few times during the season.

"Last year it was always in the back of my mind that (the shoulder) could come out. If it did I would usually have to go and sit out a series and get it to pop back in."

It was obvious to Cook the shoulder wasn't right.

"If you watched him tackle people last year there was a difference," Cook said. "He just wasn't as physical. He would get in front of some-body and wrestle him to the ground."

Was there ever a time Randolph would have considered not playing the remainder of the season and getting the shoulder fixed?

"No," he said.

As it turned out, Kell couldn't have made the playoffs without him.

Despite not being able to wrap up any ball carriers or receivers, he again was one of Cobb County's leading tacklers with 136 and added three more interceptions. An early season injury to running back Chris Gaines forced Randolph into full time duty at tailback, which led to 1,325 yards and 11 touchdowns. On special teams he was the main kick and punt returner and Randolph was usually the first player down the field on kick and punt coverage. The only plays he would come out of the game for was if the Longhorns were kicking an extra point.

As bad as the injury was, at no time did it keep the college re-cruiters away. Neither did Randolph's 4.4 speed or his 4.1 grade point average.

"I tell the recruiters this young man is a career changer," said Kell de-fensive coordinator Doug Orbaugh. "He has an established work ethic, he's academically sound and his character is beyond reproach.

"And he'll help you keep your job."

During his coaching career, Cook said he has coached some great athletes that garnered a lot of attention, including Jayson Foster while at Cherokee, Kenny McKinley at South Cobb and this year's sixth round draft pick by the Pittsburgh Steelers, Jonathan Dwyer, but none have gotten the attention of Randolph.

"I've had (Alabama coach) Nick Saban here, (then Tennessee coach) Lane Kiffin, (Stanford's) Jim Harbaugh and (Georgia's) Mark Richt," Cook said. "In one week in this office we had coaches from Georgia, Georgia Tech, Notre Dame, Ohio State, Kentucky, N.C. State, Alabama and Tennessee."

In the end, Randolph's decision came down to either Georgia Tech or Tennessee.

After making a final trip to Knoxville earlier this summer, Randolph made his choice official. Despite having to get to know new head coach Derek Dooley, and finding out what his program was going to be all about, Randolph was going to be a Volunteer.

"After having a chance to be with the new coaching staff for a few days, it all felt about the same," Randolph said.

And it didn't hurt that he was impressed with the academic side of Tennessee life. A potential business major, Randolph enjoyed touring the new 174,000-square foot, $40 million business building.

"We're still preaching academics first," said Lisa Randolph. "Football is great, but you need a good education to help become a good man and a good husband."

With the choice of college behind him, Cook pays no attention to the approximately two-dozen letters he gets at school for Randolph. He now has a special location where he keeps them all.

"I throw them away," he said. "Brian said he doesn't even want to look at them."

It's made things much easier on Randolph heading into his senior season.

"It's taken all the pressure off," he said. "Now I can enjoy my last year.

And with his surgically repaired shoulder 100 percent healthy,

Randolph is looking forward to his senior season — and getting back to the physical style of play he enjoyed as a sophomore.

"I think I'm a go-to player," Randolph said. "I like the ball or the game in my hands when the game is on the line. I want that responsibility.

COACHES TEST THEIR STAND-UP ACTS AT FOOTBALL BREAKFAST, AUGUST 10, 2010

Dr. Charlotte Stowers, the former Pope principal now serving in an interim capacity at Osborne, set the stage Wednesday morning when she compared the East Cobb Area Council's annual Pigskin Preview to the "Blue Collar Comedy Tour."

But instead of Jeff Foxworthy, Bill Engvall, Ron White and Larry the Cable Guy, the stars on stage were the six high school football coaches of east Cobb.

They didn't disappoint.

Each year, the coaches come together to tell the Chamber of Commerce members about how their teams are going to perform in the upcoming season. And it doesn't take long for the get-together to become more about the one-liners than the offensive or defensive lines.

Pope coach Matt Kemper got the first big shot in early.

"Ms. Stowers, thank you for introducing us in alphabetical order," he said. "Because that means I get to talk before Shack (Sprayberry's Billy Shackelford) and (Walton's) Rocky (Hidalgo) cause they will talk 'til lunch, and my 5-Hour Energy (drink) is about to wear off."

Shackelford fired next.

"If you are comparing us to the 'Blue Collar Comedy Tour,' I'm just afraid I'd end up being Larry the Cable Guy."

It doesn't matter what year it is, or how many coaches come and go, every coach has a sense of humor in a job where it would seem like they would be more likely to pull out their hair than crack a punchline.

"They say you can either laugh about it or cry," said Shackelford, who is entering his fourth season as the Yellow Jackets' head coach. "Laughing is more enjoyable."

Kell coach Derek Cook agreed.

"It's either insanity or a sense of humor," he said about anyone that would be willing to put a large part of their livelihood in the hands of 13-, 14-, 15-, 16- and 17-year-old kids.

Cook said he remembered a freshman game a few years ago when both the starting and backup running backs were injured and they had to put someone in the game just to fill the position. The young man started running all over the place until Cook finally yelled at him and said, "Stand next to the quarterback!"

To which the young man answered, "Which one is he?"

"At that point, I knew we were in trouble," Cook said.

Hidalgo said football forces a coach to have a sense of humor. He said players are thin-skinned and hear everything that is said about them, and everything is serious. As coaches grow older, and stay in the position longer, they build calluses and learn how to laugh at themselves and each other.

"Most of these guys, we're all at the same coaching clinics and get to spend time together. We all know we're all in the same boat, and to be honest, I root for them nine times a year when we aren't playing them."

Other gems from Wednesday's roundtable:

Cook on having his team play in next week's Corky Kell Classic at the Georgia Dome: "We told (organizer) Dave Hunter we wanted to be in it and we don't care if we play the Green Bay Packers. Well, we almost got the Green Bay Packers. We face Grayson, a top-five team that went 12-1 last year."

Shackelford as he introduced the team pastors: "Team pastors, that's plural. We don't try to get one prayer from God, we get two."

New Wheeler coach Mike Collins, who is black, responding to Shackelford: "I have to comment on coach Shack (comparing us to) the 'Blue Collar Comedy Tour.' I'm wondering, 'Who am I?'"

New Lassiter coach Jep Irwin on scrimmaging Colquitt County in the south Georgia heat this weekend: "We're scrimmaging in Moultrie and would love to have you all make the trip. If you do, bring (an electric) fan—bring 10."

Hidalgo on practicing in the heat: "We have the new turf at Walton and we can't set a foot on it because it's so hot. We sent some freshmen out there to practice and they melted into little piles of goo."

Irwin said it's gotten to a point where a sense of humor is almost a prerequisite to be a head coach these days, because a coach isn't just a coach. Now, a coach is a fundraiser, a counselor, a teacher and, in some cases, a parent. It's not just about football anymore.

"If you don't have a sense of humor," Irwin said, "you'd probably burn out."

MOUNT PARAN PREVAILS WITH COOL-TO-THE-TOUCH APPROACH, DECEMBER 14, 2014

ATLANTA—If Mount Paran Christian football coach Mitch Jordan, or any of his assistant coaches or players, felt any extra pressure to finally win a state championship for Cobb County, they certainly didn't let it show.

They also didn't leave any doubt that the 47-year title drought in the county was coming to an end.

The Eagles needed only 16 plays in the first quarter to jump to a 28-0 lead, and the eventual 49-7 rout of Eagle's Landing Christian in the

Class A private-school state championship game at the Georgia Dome was on.

Not only did it come fast, but it came easy, and it caught Jordan and his offensive coordinator, Tab Griffin, off guard.

"I looked up and it was 28-0 and there was still a couple of minutes left in the first quarter," Jordan said. "I was concerned because I didn't know if we were going to be able to maintain that (level of domination) the whole game."

Like many offensive coordinators, Griffin scripted the first 15 or so plays with the idea of finding out how the Eagle's Landing defense was going to key on running backs Dorian Walker and Taylor Trammell, and wide receiver Emoni Williams.

Griffin didn't have to go far down his list Saturday morning to find the Chargers were keying on the wrong Eagle.

On the second play from scrimmage, Walker took the handoff, went nearly untouched off the right side and escaped for a 42-yard touchdown. Griffin said it was a misdirection play, and he came back to it time and again.

"We call it our spin series," Griffin said. "We send our backs in opposite ways and it's designed to get the linebackers to react."

Oh, and did they react. They reacted just as Mount Paran had hoped.

Leading 14-0, the Eagles ran the play again. This time, Trammell took the ball and went left. He had to break a tackle, but once he did, there was nothing between him and the end zone, except 17 yards of green turf.

A third time was definitely a charm when, on the first play of the ensuing drive, Walker had a hole big enough for the entire Mount Paran community to run through. He raced for 50 of his game-high 215 yards and it was 28-0.

The Eagles scored twice more before the half and took a 42-7 lead into the locker room.

"Never in a million years did I expect us to score that fast," Griffin said. "Never did I expect it to be 42-7 at the half, or even 30-0 at the end of the game. But I felt I got in the zone and the kids got in a zone."

For good measure, the spin series made Eagle's Landing's heads spin one more time.

Walker scored on a 21-yard run in the third quarter. It was the only scoring in the second half and the Eagles, in their seventh year as a program, officially lifted a 47-year old albatross off Cobb County's neck.

"We wanted to do it for Cobb County," Jordan said. "It was one of the motivating factors."

Jordan also looked at it as a way to thank many of the people who have helped him since he arrived at Mount Paran in 2008.

"There are so many great coaches in the county that have helped me out so much," he said. "(Former Harrison coach) Bruce (Cobleigh) is a mentor. (Former Walton offensive coordinator) Tripp Allen and (Former Walton coach) Ed Dudley came and talked to our team, and Rocky (Hidalgo) is one of my close friends."

In fact, Hidalgo, the former Walton coach who was the last from the county to lead a team to the state championship game when his Raiders played for the title in 2011, was one of the first people to congratulate Jordan as he came off the field.

Of course, if there's one coach who may have earned a little payback, it was Mount Paran's offensive line coach, Kenny Palmer, who's been an assistant in Cobb County for more than three decades of his 41-year coaching career. Palmer said he had never been on a staff that had gotten past the state quarterfinals until this year.

"I guess it feels better than I expected," Palmer said of finally being able to be on a championship-winning staff. "I don't think it's sunk in yet. I'm kind of numb."

But it was his offensive line that, along with Griffin, Walker and

Trammell, found the zone, the end zone and ran the spin series to perfection.

They also helped allow Mount Paran to finish the season a perfect 14-0, and that 0 has a little more significance. Thanks to the Eagles, it's now 0 years since Cobb County has won a state championship.

MORGAN BRINGS BUSINESSLIKE APPROACH TO MARIETTA, FEBRUARY 13, 2016

MARIETTA—He strolled across the stage in his dark-blue pinstripe suit, complete with white shirt, red power tie and pocket square. During a nearly 30-minute PowerPoint presentation, he produced an impressive profit and loss statement, and a detailed plan on how the company was going to proceed in the future.

By the time he was done, the shareholders seemed enthusiastic about reinvesting in the company on a long-term basis.

But this wasn't the CEO or president of a company leading a stockholders' meeting. This was new Marietta football coach Richard Morgan holding court at a meet-and-greet held in the school's performing arts center Wednesday evening.

He had everyone's attention.

"You have greatness inside of you," Morgan told the players. "You just have to have it pulled out of you."

Morgan was more than impressive. He won many of the players over as soon as he posted his credentials on the screen from his tenure at Oscar Smith High School in Chesapeake, Virginia.

- A win-loss record of 164-20 since 2002 in Virginia's highest classification
- Two state championships, two runner-up finishes, semifinal

teams seven of the last nine seasons and 12 straight district championships

- Nationally ranked 10 of the last 12 years, with 71 all-state players.

Morgan wasn't bragging. He expertly pivoted into the reason he wanted everyone to know why he was telling them this.

"I'm using these to make an impact," Morgan said. "Before I got there, Oscar Smith had played 48 years and never made the playoffs. There were 36 players on the varsity roster, and 18 of them were in summer school trying to get eligible.

"Marietta is nowhere near (the depths) where that program was."

Morgan is no stranger to the area. In his time as a young assistant at Tri-Cities and St. Pius X, before he moved on to Virginia, Morgan lived in Marietta for six years. He understands what the Blue Devil football team means in the community, and he knows the job ahead of him.

"He's an amazing football coach," said Scott Brunet, a longtime assistant of Morgan's at Oscar Smith before he came to Marietta last season as the defensive line coach under former head coach Scott Burton. "He lives for the challenge. He wants to do what he did at Oscar Smith again. He wants to prove to himself that he can do it again."

Brunet said Morgan is very much the CEO-like coach he appears to be. It showed in the detail he puts into his PowerPoint presentation, and some of the words and phrases he uses.

During the evening, Morgan showed a detailed schedule—starting from the time he officially steps on campus March 1 through spring practice and summer workouts, all the way to Aug. 1, when teams can don pads for the first time.

He didn't quote Vince Lombardi or Bear Bryant. Rather, he used a quote attributed to the Rev. Martin Luther King Jr.—"The fierce urgency of now."

While King's fierce urgency was how the Civil Rights movement could create immediate political change, Morgan used it as a way to summarize what he expects to see on the field this coming season.

"This is not going to be a 10-year rebuilding project," he said. "We have a fierce urgency now."

Morgan showed that over the last nine years, his teams averaged 41 points per game. He said he will tailor the offense to his personnel, but his teams will be aggressive, attack and play up-tempo. Morgan showed that his Oscar Smith quarterbacks threw for an average of 3,200 yards and 38 touchdowns per season, and the running backs ran for 2,000 yards and another 30 scores.

Morgan's teams allowed an average of nine points a game over the last nine years. His defenses will be relentless, play fast and be physical.

"And we have more athletes here than the school where I just left," he said.

In order to be part of the new brand of Marietta football, Morgan explained what the players would need to do in the classroom.

He told parents there would be bi-weekly grade checks and study halls. He said the players have been given a gift by being able to play the game and earn a quality education in a place like Marietta High School, and they will do projects to give back to the community.

"The goal is to be eligible to go to college," Morgan said. "Not to be eligible to play football."

Morgan even showed his equation for determining a player's heart: $E+R=O$. Events plus reaction equals outcome.

As Morgan sees it, there are going to be events with an outcome every day. How a person reacts to those events will determine that outcome.

"If it's important to you, you will find a way," he said. "If it's not important to you, you will find an excuse."

According to those who covered Morgan's Oscar Smith teams at the Virginian-Pilot newspaper, Morgan has a fiery personality that can sometimes rub people the wrong way, but he goes out of his way to preach family and accountability. Loyalty would have to be considered, too, as all but one coach on Morgan's former staff was a former player of his.

Morgan showed some of that fire Wednesday night when he asked the players, parents and other community members to join him in an exercise at the beginning of his presentation, and then again at the end. He wanted them to be fired up and to answer his question that way.

"Marietta, how do you feel?"

"FIRED UP!" the crowd yelled in response.

Morgan will never have another chance to make a good first impression. He doesn't need one. Everyone seemed to leave the Marietta auditorium with high expectations.

Now, all he has to do is meet them.

FAMILY WAS THE THEME AS THE LIFE OF MARIETTA ICON WHO 'WAS SO MUCH TO SO MANY' WAS CELEBRATED, JUNE 30, 2018

Family. It's a simple word, but it could be the most important word of all.

That's how it was to former Marietta High School football coach James "Friday" Richards, and it showed Friday night as nearly 2,000 members of his extended family came to Northcutt Stadium to show what Richards meant to them.

"Family. That was a word I heard from coach Friday more than any other," said Marietta athletic director Paul Hall, who played for and coached alongside Richards with the Blue Devils. "Everyone that came in contact with him was made to feel like family.

"Coach was so much to so many."

So, quite fittingly on the same field where Richards had gained his notoriety, Friday night brought Friday's "family" back together.

After Richards died unexpectedly last weekend, the gathering provided a celebration of life that was befitting of someone who spent nearly five decades in and around the school he loved so much.

The Marietta native first came to prominence as a player on the football field, where he built long-lasting friendships, but it was his personal touch, kindness and philosophy off the field that made him the person everyone was there to remember.

Richards was a builder of young men and women. When someone needed help, he or she knew they could turn to him. It could have been as simple as a ride home, a meal or a word of encouragement.

In the case of former Marietta running back Terrance Huey, it was saving his life.

Richards took Huey in off the street and kept him from a life of crime and drugs after he lost his biological father at a young age. The first day he met Richards, Huey said, he knew he found his father, and he forever referred to Richards as "Dad."

Huey wasn't the only one.

"I was one of many to be helped, groomed and prepared for life by coach Friday," former Marietta and Tennessee running back Derrick Tinsley said. "The only thing bigger than coach Friday's smile was his heart. The only thing better than his hugs was his unconditional love."

That unconditional love had no bounds. It was for everyone.

"Family," Hall said. "He made everyone feel like part of his family."

One of Richards' favorite sayings was, "Be somebody."

It wasn't something original. His mentor, former Lemon Street and Marietta coach Ben Wilkins, uttered it first, but Richards made it his own.

Rose Jones, who was a track and field athlete of Richards' at Marietta before going on to compete at Georgia Tech, presented a question to all comers Friday as she held up a relay baton that belonged to Richards.

"This baton symbolizes the relay of life," Jones said. "A long time ago, coach Ben Wilkins passed it on to coach Friday. Tonight, it has to be passed on. Are you up to the challenge? The best way we can honor coach Friday is to lend a helping hand to our brothers and sisters of our community. In other words, be somebody."

Following the ceremony, Richards' extended family continued the reunion.

Former players and coaches milled around the field, with handshakes and high-fives. There were also big hugs and plenty of tears.

While it wasn't the reason everyone wanted to get together, in typical Richards way, it seemed to make everyone's bond a little tighter, and it further showed why this one man had such an impact.

For the last few years, Richards had been an assistant coach at White-field Academy. The current members of the Wolfpack football team were all in attendance, and John Hunter said Richards had a similar effect on them.

"It was more than just the game," said Hunter, who spent the last two years as Whitefield's head coach before sliding back into an assistant's role for the upcoming season. "His passion was all about people. He used the platform of football to reach people. It was important for our kids to see that the last couple of years.

"It didn't take long to become a Friday fan."

It didn't, and the people of Marietta, Cobb County and everyone else who had the opportunity to know Richards is forever better for it.

WE'VE REACHED A BITTERSWEET TIME OF THE HIGH SCHOOL FOOTBALL SEASON, NOVEMBER 7, 2019

Last week, Marietta's Harrison Bailey became the fifth quarterback in state history to throw for 10,000 yards in a career.

The Tennessee commit will likely move into fourth all-time this week when the Blue Devils travel to Kennesaw Mountain to close the regular season. It will leave him behind a Who's Who of the position as it comes to Georgia high school football—Trevor Lawrence, Deshaun Watson and Jake Fromm.

Bailey already owns nearly every Cobb County passing record, and he will set marks that are going to be hard to reach going forward. Eventually, somebody will, but we will be able to look back and say "remember when..."

Up to now, the 6-foot-4, 217-pound four-star prospect has given Marietta fans plenty of memories. The Blue Devils and Bailey know they have at least two more games to play. If things go right, it could stretch to six, but that won't be the case for many of the players who could see their football careers end Friday as the regular season comes to a close.

On any team, there are the players who are really good, but, for whatever reason, don't get a chance to play in college. It won't be surprising that, for many of them, it will be hard to take that jersey off for the last time.

Many of those players are names we may never have heard of or written about, but for every Bailey, Arik Gilbert, Jamil Burroughs, Javon Baker, Myles Murphy and Victor Pless—some of the players who will continue their careers at Power Five schools—they have 10 or 15 unsung teammates who pushed them along the way and helped to get them there.

Those are the real players who need to be commended. They are the glue, and they are the ones who make the others look good.

Over the next few weeks, every player's season will eventually come to a close. In the end, only eight teams across the state will get to smile and say they won their last game in December as state champions.

I don't know if any Cobb County teams will make it that far this year, but I am grateful that I've had the opportunity to watch this year's seniors grow up and become young men. And there have been more than a few who have become some of my favorites.

Mount Paran Christian quarterback Niko Vangarelli is one.

The 6-2, 220-pound dual-threat has been Mr. Everything for the Eagles this season. Through eight games, he has run for 1,258 yards and 13 touchdowns, and he has thrown for 1,209 yards and nine touchdowns.

Vangarelli joins a small club of county quarterbacks over the last decade—Walker's Joseph Vose (2017), South Cobb's Kylil Carter (2014), McEachern's Ty Clemons (2013), Pope's Holland Frost (2010) and Hillgrove's Gage Henry (2010)—who have run and thrown for more than 1,000 yards in the same season.

Of course, there is a difference between Vangarelli and most of those others. The Princeton commit also starts on defense and, for good measure, has added 28 tackles, a sack and an interception.

A couple years ago, when Justin Fields was starring at Harrison, David Roberts was just beginning to get a sense of what he could be. Now, as a senior, he has run for 825 yards and eight touchdowns on only 88 carries.

Roberts is one good game away from his second 1,000-yard rushing season, and he will go over 2,500 yards for his career at the same time. The 5-11, 200-pounder has a number of offers from FCS programs, and wherever he decides to go, that program is going to get a steal.

Over the last decade, it seems like Cobb County has been at the forefront of redefining what it means to be a high school kicker. It was not that long ago when coaches were just trying to find out if there was someone on the roster who could make an extra point.

Former Sprayberry standout Rodrigo Blankenship is forcing everyone to "respect the specs" at Georgia, and he will soon be in the NFL. Marietta's Ian Shannon, who went on to punt at Auburn, may have had the strongest leg I've ever seen. Following in their footsteps is current Allatoona kicker Jude Kelley.

Kelley is considered one of the top, if not the top, kicking prospect in the country by the recruiting services. This season, he is 13-of-15 on field goals and has made all 29 of his extra points. He set an Allatoona record at the beginning of the year with a 54-yard field goal, and he is the county's leading punter, averaging 47.5 yards an attempt.

With at least two games to play and hopefully more, Kelley is three field goals away from equaling Shannon's county record of 16 set in 2013.

I'm going to miss seeing what Hillgrove quarterback Matthew Mc-Cravy does each week. In a region that saw Kennesaw Mountain's Jarrett Guest head to Coastal Carolina last year, Bailey to Tennessee this year and McEachern's Carlos Del Rio-Wilson to Florida next year, McCravy has found ways to outplay all of them at one time or another.

Pebblebrook's Quincy Miller has put up 24.5 sacks and more than 220 tackles over the last two seasons. He is going to wreak havoc in the Sun Belt Conference for former Lassiter coach Chip Lindsey at Troy.

There's also Walton's K.D. Stokes, Lassiter's Jack Ferguson, Walker's Jake Tasman, Pope's Will Zegers, Allatoona's Asante Das, North Cobb Christian's Ryan Pruitt and Sprayberry's Marlon Krakue, and the list goes on and on and on.

You seniors have helped make Cobb County football what it is. It has been a pleasure to cover you during your time in school, and I wish you luck in your future endeavors.

And for the fans of Cobb County high school football, we say thank you.

COBB IS THE KING OF HIGH SCHOOL FOOTBALL, DECEMBER 15, 2019

I like to tell the story that one of the first things I did after becoming sports editor of the Marietta Daily Journal was to deal with National Signing Day.

It was February of 2007 and we invited all of the Division I football signees to the MDJ offices for pictures and interviews. That year, they all fit into our small conference room. There were six players who were going on to play big-time college football.

That 2006 high school football season, six Cobb County teams made the playoffs—Campbell, North Cobb, South Cobb, Walton, Wheeler and Whitefield Academy. Of those six, only Campbell advanced to the second round. The season in the county was completely done by Thanksgiving.

That's not the case any more.

Cobb County is the king of high school football in Georgia in 2019.

Let that sink in for a minute. Cobb County is the king of high school football in the state of Georgia.

It's been a long time coming, and there are a lot of people who likely thought it would never get here. While the county has dominated in nearly every sport other than football—see 2019 volleyball champions Allatoona and Walton, softball champion Pope, boys cross country winners Walton and Harrison, along with the Walton and Hillgrove girls (not a bad fall season by the way)—the gridiron always seemed to be ruled by south Georgia or Gwinnett County. Over the last 20 years, Gwinnett and south Georgia took the trophy home in the two highest classifications a combined 27 times.

Not this year.

Harrison and Allatoona provided the county with a no-lose situation on Friday night. It was the first time two Cobb teams had squared off in a football state championship game. It was too bad that the weather didn't cooperate to allow more fans to be there, but the Hoyas took care of their business and completed the first 15-0 season in Cobb County history. Plus, it was only the second undefeated season in county history joining Mount Paran Christian, which went 14-0 in its title season of 2014.

I would also be remiss if I did not mention the best moment of the weekend came out of Harrison's victory. It was when coach Matt Dickmann dedicated the win to former Hoyas coach, and program founder, Bruce Cobleigh, who passed away two years ago. Pure class.

Marietta kept things rolling on Saturday. The quick passing game and getting players in space had the Blue Devils offense going through the Lowndes defense like a hot knife through butter in the first half. It allowed them to build a lead big enough to withstand the Vikings' comeback and give Marietta its first state title since 1967.

The Blue Devils air attack reminded me of the offense that former Lassiter, and current Troy University coach Chip Lindsey first brought to the county in 2008. His offense was an eye opener and showed what could happen when a team's best athletes could get the ball without anyone around them for a few yards. Soon others followed suit. That change, and a group of better coaches, finally dragged the county into the modern day of high school football. Gone was everyone lining up and looking at three yards and a cloud of dust.

For the fifth year in a row, the county had more 1,500 yard passers (9) than it had 1,000 yard rushers (8). And after watching Marietta's Harrison Bailey throw for more than 4,200 yards this season, moving the ball through the air is going to become even more commonplace.

Wednesday is the first of two National Signing Days for football. We are likely to see 15—maybe 20—players sign National Letters of Intent, not only with Division I programs, but with the Power 5 variety. By the time we get to the second signing day, we will likely have another 20-plus sign to play Group of 5 and FCS.

The way Cobb County high school football has advanced over the last decade, it's hard to imagine it slowing down now. In 2014, we were wondering if the county would ever break its then 47-year drought without a state championship. Mount Paran finally gave us the answer. Allatoona followed the following year, and now we have four in the last five years.

That includes two in 2019.

Congratulations to all the players and coaches who suited up and brought us a year's worth of excitement.

For this season, Cobb County is the king of Georgia high school football.

It won't be the last.

BASEBALL

ATLANTA VERY NEARLY GOT ANOTHER KIND OF 'BIG CHICKEN', JUNE 27, 2015

SAN DIEGO—The Famous San Diego Chicken has become a pop culture icon, performing his act at ballparks around the country for more than 40 years. But Ted Giannoulas, the 61-year-old comedian who brings the chicken to life, said he was close to calling a different city home.

How does the Famous Atlanta Chicken sound?

Giannoulas was the keynote speaker Thursday during the Associated Press Sports Editors' annual summer conference and said he almost called Atlanta home after a generous offer by former Braves owner Ted Turner.

It was the mid- to late 1970s, when Turner was building WTBS into a national superstation and had plans for a fledgling cable news outlet that would be called CNN. The Braves were challenging the Cubs in becoming America's team, having joined Chicago in having the majority of its games broadcast nationwide.

Giannoulas was a student at San Diego State University and donned the Chicken suit as a promotional stunt for KGB-FM in San Diego. At the initial event, the Chicken was to hand out Easter eggs at the zoo, but it wasn't long before Giannoulas' reputation as an entertainer grew and he was working San Diego Padres games.

Turner liked the routine and hired the Chicken to come and enter-tain Braves fans for a weekend — only, Giannoulas said, Turner had eyes on a much bigger and longer relationship. The Braves' owner wanted to hire him full-time.

However, the job offer was unique and not what Giannoulas expect-ed.

Upon arriving at the old Atlanta-Fulton County Stadium and en-tertaining the fans for a few innings, Giannoulas said he was heading down the aisle to Turner's seats when the owner met him halfway and said, "Come with me."

Giannoulas said he was excited with the meeting and expected to be escorted to Turner's office or owner's suite.

Instead, the unlikely pair went to the men's room.

But it was there that Turner, after completing his personal business, turned his focus toward Giannoulas. Turner offered the then-19-year-old student $50,000 to come to the Deep South.

"He had called the Padres and offered to give them the backup catch-er they needed," Giannoulas said. "They offered to trade Biff Pocoroba to the Padres for me.

"They told (Turner), 'We can't trade him. He doesn't work for us. We don't even pay him.'"

Giannoulas was still employed by the San Diego radio station.

He was floored with the offer from Turner, who wanted him to start the next day. Despite making only minimum wage at the station, Gi-annoulas, who still lived with his parents, wanted to go home and talk to his family about the opportunity first.

"We have phones here," Giannoulas said Turner told him. "Give 'em a call."

Giannoulas went home anyway, but as Turner often did in business, he wouldn't take no for an answer.

"When I got home, the offer was $100,000 a year," Giannoulas said.

He said Turner had big plans for him, including giving him his own TV show on WTBS. In the end though, the Chicken's heart couldn't leave the West Coast.

Years later, Giannoulas said Turner told him he admired the decision.

"He said he had a lot of respect for what I did," Giannoulas said.

The Chicken did end up on TV for a number of years in the '80s, working on "The Baseball Bunch," a Major League Baseball-produced children's program with Hall of Famers Johnny Bench and Tommy Lasorda. But what Giannoulas has mainly been known for is his antics on the field, routinely working 180 days a year during baseball season, going ballpark to ballpark.

Now, in his fifth decade as the Chicken, Giannoulas' schedule has been pared down a little bit, and he isn't as spry as he used to be, but he's still out there entertaining the masses. It's because of the reaction he gets from the crowd, and because he can touch the lives of so many people.

He has no regrets from not taking Turner's offer, and it begs the question. What would have happened to the likes of Chief Noc-A-Homa, Rally and Homer?

It's a question that can't be answered, and one that Biff Pocoroba is probably thankful for. Because how would you explain being traded for a chicken?

COACH MAC'S NEW HOME: WHEELER ICON STARTS ANEW, MINUS A PIECE OF HIS HEART, MARCH 27, 2011

Every day, Dave McDonald shows up at the ballpark around 1 p.m. and begins to prepare the field for that day's practice or game.

It's the same routine he's followed for 30 years, but this season is different.

He's no longer working on the field named after him at Wheeler, the school where he won 483 career games and was named to the Georgia Dugout Club and National High School Baseball Coaches halls of fame.

Not only is McDonald no longer at Wheeler, he's no longer a head coach. As a pitching coach, he is now trying to turn Mount Paran Christian's park into a new field of dreams, and the Eagles' pitching staff into a force to be reckoned with.

Through 15 games, Mount Paran is 9-6 with a roster made up of nearly all freshmen and sophomores. It's led by a group of young pitchers who are not only learning the finer points of the game but, according to head coach Harvey Cochran, are showing the potential necessary to play on the next level, thanks to McDonald.

"Coach Mac has done an amazing job with these young guys," Cochran said. "If they keep progressing, we have some that will play in Division I."

Having the opportunity to mold the Eagles' pitching staff is gratifying to McDonald, but that doesn't mean he's not thinking about the place he called home since the early 1980s.

"It's taken a while to get used to the new royal blue and white uniform," he said. "I'm so used to putting on navy and gold. I spent 30 years at Wheeler and, in a lot of ways, my heart is still there."

So much so that he continues to talk with the Wildcats' new coach, Jeff Milton, a few times a week.

"We stay in touch. I knew, with (Milton) being new, he would have questions, and I am trying to help him as much as I can."

McDonald was forced out of his position as a coach and physical education teacher at Wheeler at the end of the last school year. He was one of the casualties of the Cobb County School District's cost-cutting decision to eliminate more than 450 "49-percent" employees—workers who had retired, but were rehired by the district as a part-time teacher—to help eliminate a $137 million budget shortfall for the 2011 fiscal year.

In all, the district initially eliminated more than 1,000 teaching positions. Some, including a few of the part-time coaches, eventually were hired back. McDonald wasn't one of those fortunate ones, and it's something that still stays with him each day.

"I'm not bitter—just disappointed," he said. "I'm disappointed, not only for me, but for all the teachers who lost their jobs."

Initially, McDonald did not expect to miss his classroom work as much as he has, but he misses the daily interaction with the students who weren't his baseball players.

"That's where you get to know the students," he said, "and where you get to know each other. I miss that a lot.

"It's disappointing, and sure, I'm older, but I still felt like I had a lot to give."

As it turned out, McDonald wasn't the only one feeling that way.

Once the 2010 season was over, he had a number of different opportunities to choose from. He had the option to coach small-college baseball, work as a scout or go to join one of Wheeler's principal east Cobb rivals.

Kell coach Donnie English—part of the triumvirate of Cobb County coaching greats that includes Cochran and McDonald, and one of the part-timers who returned to his post—approached McDonald about joining his staff as pitching coach, but out of loyalty, he turned down the offer.

"I didn't want to have to compete against Wheeler," McDonald said. "Kell is one of the premier programs in the county, but I didn't want to have to go back (to Wheeler) with a different team."

Then entered Cochran, himself a 35-year veteran coach, who tried to convince McDonald through much of last summer that Mount Paran was the right place to go.

Finally, Cochran said he wore his old friend down.

"We were at a Dugout Club meeting in October and I just went over and said, 'You going to come help us or not?'"

McDonald relented, creating a version of baseball's "Odd Couple." Combined, the coaches have won more than 1,100 games over their careers, but McDonald said on-field success was one of the few things the men had in common.

"I like things organized. Everything has a set time on the schedule," McDonald said. "Harvey, he likes to fly by the seat of his pants."

Initially, the coaches said it took awhile to get used to each other's style, but now that the roles are defined, everything is falling into place.

When McDonald agreed to join the Eagles' staff, Cochran completely turned over the pitching staff to him and vowed to stay out of his new assistant's way. And to ensure it stays that way, the men developed a system to make sure they don't step on each other's game plan.

When Mount Paran is at bat, Cochran stands near the on-deck circle and McDonald is on the other end of the dugout. When the Eagles' defense is in the field, Cochran and McDonald switch places.

"That's why we did it the way we did," Cochran said. "We gave up our egos for the better of the kids."

As the season continues, the arrangement seems to be working. Heading into Tuesday's game against Darlington, Mount Paran has won four in a row, eight of 11 and has a stranglehold on second place in Region 6A, two games behind Walker. The Eagles also have the knowledge that they have to play the Wolverines twice before the end of the season, which means they control their fate on the way toward a possible region title.

And that, more than anything, justifies Cochran's wish to have McDonald join the staff.

"The Cobb County system messed up," Cochran said. "You always try to get somebody like (McDonald), and when you can, you don't turn that down. You would have to be crazy to turn down his services."

In the end, Cobb County's loss is turning out to be Mount Paran's gain.

RETIREMENT DESERVED TO BE BETTER FOR MCMURTRY, JUNE 12, 2011

Gen. Douglas MacArthur, in his farewell address to Congress in 1951, quoted an old Army ballad, saying, "Old soldiers never die, they just fade away."

The same can be said for old coaches.

There was no fuss or fanfare for Mickey McMurtry this spring when he retired after 26 years at Lassiter High School.

He was happy to have a low-key farewell.

Too bad he didn't get the chance to retire the way he had wanted.

This was the year he was to go out as an American government teacher AND baseball coach.

Two years ago, McMurtry was reportedly relieved of his coaching duties after run-ins with then-principal Chris Shaw over personnel issues.

No public reason has been given for the move, other than Shaw saying he wanted to "take the baseball program in another direction." The decision just didn't make much sense.

In 17 years as the Trojans' head coach, McMurtry compiled a record of 537-156, seven region titles, seven trips to the state finals and two state titles in 1999 and 2006. In '99, Lassiter also won the national championship nod from Baseball America and Collegiate Baseball.

"I'm still disappointed in how it ended," McMurtry said earlier this week.

But as quickly as McMurtry's coaching career at Lassiter ended, that's how fast he disappeared from baseball altogether.

As proud as he was of his former assistant, Scott Kelly, leading Lassiter back to the state finals in 2010, McMurtry stayed as far away as possible. Not because he didn't care for his players, coaches or program—it was actually just the opposite.

McMurtry didn't want to be a distraction, and he's made sure it stayed that way.

In the two years since he coached his last game, McMurtry has seen less than one inning of high school baseball.

"I was out walking my dog and went over to see Nelson Ward hit against Pope," he said. "Other than that, when I was done, I was done."

Surprisingly, with only a couple of exceptions, McMurtry said he hasn't really missed the game.

"Sure, I miss my colleagues," he said. "And I miss the playoffs. But I don't miss practicing in 30-degree weather in February."

McMurtry arrived at Lassiter in 1985 as a social studies teacher and it was then when football coach Dexter Wood brought him on his staff to be an assistant coach. Four years later, McMurtry moved into his two permanent residences at the school—in the classroom as the head of the social studies department, and into the dugout at the baseball field.

As he was cleaning out his desk and files during the last few days of school, the 55-year-old McMurtry said he really started to reflect back on his entire teaching career. He then found something that put everything in the proper perspective—a photo of the Lassiter baseball facilities from when he was an assistant under coach Jeff Guy.

"People forget, the stadium wasn't always like this," McMurtry said. "We started out with a chain-link fence back there, and all the big pine trees you see now were just saplings."

And there was one other added feature.

"There was a big barn back there you could see plain as day," he said. "The farmer let us paint it burgundy and we put Lassiter baseball on the side of it."

The facilities then became McMurtry's passion. As they developed, he made sure there was never a tuft of grass out of place, the infield was always smooth and the bases and base lines extra white.

McMurtry knew the vision he, the school and the booster club want-ed for the baseball complex, but as much time as he put in to making everything look good, he refuses to take more than a little credit.

"I did my part," McMurtry said, "but it was the booster club, the parents and Guerry Baldwin and the East Cobb (Baseball) people. There were hundreds of people that had a hand in the facility. I was just the caretaker."

It couldn't have been a coincidence, though, that, shortly after Mc-Murtry was named head coach in 1992, the Trojans became a perennial playoff team and state title contender.

After 17 years as coach, McMurtry conceded there are a few things he may have liked to do differently—a conversation here, a coachable moment there—but as far as on the field, he has no regrets—not even pitching to Jeff Francoeur in the state championship series against Parkview in 2002.

"He was just an unbelievable player," McMurtry said of the future major-leaguer, who hit a number of long home runs in the series and even recorded the save as a pitcher in the decisive game. "What we should have done was probably throw the ball right down the middle of the plate. (Francoeur) was known as a pretty good bad-ball hitter, and you should have seen some of the pitches he hit out."

The last few years McMurtry served as coach, detractors began to surface, criticizing the way he ran the Lassiter program. The argument was, with all the talent the Trojans had, why didn't they win more than two state titles under the coach's watch.

For those who think that way, they don't realize how hard it is just to advance to seven state championship series.

"You get to the finals and there is another good team in the other dugout," McMurtry said.

In those failed trips to the finals, Lassiter may have been the other teams' equal, but the Trojans never had a difference-maker like Marlon

Byrd, Stephen Drew or Francoeur in their dugout. Sprayberry, Lowndes and Parkview did.

Over the last two baseball-free years, McMurtry refocused his energies in other areas. He spent time walking his dog, a black lab named Cooper, took up bike riding and, as he's proud to claim, "My yard looks better than it ever has."

More importantly, however, McMurtry feels like the last two years he became a better teacher. It was what he called an "interesting dynamic" that finally made him make the decision to retire.

"Man, I'm 40 years older than the kids I'm teaching," he said. "Now I'm even 10 years older than their parents."

McMurtry will never say never when it comes to coaching again, but it's going to have to be a good offer to get him back to the bench.

For now, his days as a head coach and teacher are likely over.

"You just have a strong sense when it's time to retire," he said. "I'm young enough to still do something else. I just don't know what that is yet."

CHIEF WAHOO IS BASEBALL FOR ME, JANUARY 31, 2018

On Monday, the Cleveland Indians announced they would no longer wear their Chief Wahoo logo on uniforms and caps beginning in 2019.

I understand the reasoning, but the idea is painful to me. The red-faced Indian caricature with the blue feather in its headband is offensive to many Native Americans.

Many people just call it racist.

Major League Baseball commissioner Rob Manfred has been asking Indians owner Paul Dolan to consider making the change for the last few years. Manfred finally got his wish, but that sure doesn't make me feel any better.

For those of you who know me, I am an unabashed Cleveland sports fan. I've lived through Browns seasons that ended with historic games that have their own nicknames—"Red-right 88," "The Drive," "The Fumble."

While I have gotten a respite with LeBron James leading the Cavaliers to a championship two years ago, there is still "The Shot" that was put up by Michael Jordan to add to the daggers through the heart.

And then there are the Indians, the team the movie "Major League" made famous. The one that went 100-44 in a strike-shortened 1995 season, only to see their title dreams doused by the pitching of Glavine, Maddux and Smoltz (perhaps you've heard of them?). Then, two years later, it was at the hands of the too-new-to-win Florida Marlins franchise.

Fast-forward two decades, and it became the team—led by manager Terry Francona and pitcher Corey Kluber—that won games with smoke and mirrors to reach Game 7 of the 2016 World Series, which then followed that up with an American League-record 22-game winning streak last season.

Here's the rub for me and countless other Indians fans.

The baseball on the field is what Chief Wahoo represented. I never looked at the logo as a denigrating symbol. I saw it as a cartoon that made me smile, and not once did I ever compare it to or associate it with any actual Native American tribe.

I don't think I'm alone in this. It's why a poll on Cleveland.com showed 73 percent of fans saying getting rid of the logo is a mistake.

Walter Goldbach drew the first Chief 70 years ago. He never meant it to become a political flashpoint. He drew it for then-owner Bill Veeck, who was looking for a new logo. Veeck loved it and put it on the uniform in time to see the team win the 1948 World Series, and it's been a part of the fabric of the club ever since.

A few months before Goldbach died in 2016, he told a TV station in Cleveland, "You look at Chief Wahoo and all he wants to tell you is, 'Come on. Let's win a few games. I've got a smile on my face.' That's the way I see him."

To me, Chief Wahoo meant a day at the ballpark—Cleveland Municipal Stadium and then Jacobs Field, which is now Progressive Field—with a scorecard in hand, along with a cold beverage and a hot dog with the famous Cleveland Stadium Mustard.

It meant Frank Robinson, Boog Powell and Duane Kiper in the blood-red uniforms of the 1970s with the "crooked C" cap. It meant "Super Joe" Charboneau, Andre Thornton and Len Barker of the early '80s, along with Corey Snyder, Greg Swindell and the misguided Sports Illustrated prediction of the 1987 Indians winning the World Series—before they went 61-101.

The Chief also meant the '90s teams with Kenny Lofton, Sandy Alomar, Albert Belle, Manny Ramirez, Omar Vizquel and first-ballot Hall of Famer Jim Thome, who was elected with the Braves' Chipper Jones last week.

Thome, who was my favorite player, hit 612 home runs in his career for six different teams, but he will go into the Hall this summer wearing an Indians cap. It will be interesting to see if the cap has Chief Wahoo on it, because there was no "Block C" logo—the Indians' primary logo since 2013—when Thome was mashing most of his team-record 337 home runs.

For me, the Chief has long meant baseball in northeast Ohio. I know he gets one last go around this season, but I still can't help but feel like I am losing another piece of my childhood.

I'm sure that many Braves fans thought the same thing when the organization retired Chief Noc-A-Homa and their old "screaming Indian" logo.

Hopefully, the Indians can have the same kind of success without Wahoo as the Braves did once they dropped Noc-A-Homa. It was not long after that Atlanta won 14 straight division titles and a World Series. Now, enough time has passed that anybody under the age of 40 barely has a memory of him.

Soon, that will be the same with Chief Wahoo.

For my reasons, I will miss him.

Times change. I realize getting rid of the logo is the right thing to do, but just because it's right doesn't mean I have to like it.

BRAVES PUT ORGANIZATION, FANS IN BAD LIGHT WITH TOMAHAWKS, OCTOBER 11, 2019

The Atlanta Braves organization made a statement Wednesday, and it had nothing to do with the team's performance on the field.

Whether they knew it or not, those in the Braves' front office threw themselves and their fan base under the bus and painted the team in a bad light.

It stemmed from the decision not to divvy out the more than 41,000 foam tomahawks in the seats before the Braves faced the St. Louis in Wednesday's decisive fifth game of the National League Division Series.

As the teams played the first two games of the series at SunTrust Park, a Cardinals beat writer asked reliever Ryan Helsley for his thoughts on the Braves' tradition of the Tomahawk Chop—the rallying cry copied from Florida State when former Seminole football star Deion Sanders played for the Braves in the 1990s.

Helsley, a member of the Cherokee Nation, answered honestly, saying he found the Chop to be "disappointing" and "disrespectful."

Before Wednesday's game, the Braves released the following statement:

"Out of respect for the concerns expressed by Mr. Helsley, we will take several efforts to reduce the Tomahawk Chop during our in-ball-park presentation today. Among other things, these steps include not distributing foam tomahawks to each seat and not playing the accompanying music or using Chop-related graphics when Mr. Helsley is in the game. As stated earlier, we will continue to evaluate how we activate elements of our brand, as well as the overall in-game experience. We look forward to a continued dialogue with those in the Native American community after the postseason concludes."

With the statement, the Braves agreed with Helsley. They said the fans were insensitive, and from the organization's standpoint, they realized the Tomahawk Chop and everything and everyone associated with it was wrong.

No one asked the Braves to make changes prior to the game. Members of the organization said it came from internal discussions.

If you have a fan tradition, you either do it or you don't. You can't limit the Chop to just a few times during the game. And if you aren't going to give out the foam tomahawks to all the fans, then don't allow them to be sold on game days in the team shop.

To do it the way they did, it appeared to be a knee-jerk reaction that put the Braves, their fans and anyone else affiliated with the team in a bad light, and it could have caused an even bigger problem.

Imagine what might have happened if Helsley was brought into a close game. As the face of the issue, fans would have directed their displeasure at him. There may have been a scene, or worse.

In full disclosure, I am a Cleveland Indians fan. This past season was the first the Indians did not have Chief Wahoo — the team's toothy, grinning mascot — on their caps and uniforms, or used by the team in any of its advertising, promotions or social media campaigns.

I wasn't happy when the Indians did away with the Chief, because it was like losing a part of my childhood. I never considered it offensive. I still think of it as a cartoon that meant it was summer and my favorite baseball team was playing.

If the Chop is lost, it will affect a lot of Braves fans the same way the Chief affected me.

That being said, what the Braves did Wednesday was wrong.

The Indians negotiated with Major League Baseball for years to bring the end to Chief Wahoo.

Like that, the Braves' situation is something that should be determined in the offseason, not two hours before the gates are opened. If the organization truly believes that a change needs to be made, then make it. Eliminate the Chop, and do away with the social media hashtag, #ChopOn, change the name of the Chop House and take the tomahawks off the uniforms.

If you make a change, do it because it's the right thing to do, but don't leave your fans hanging during a nationally televised playoff game.

THIS AND THAT

A SUPER BOWL ONLY A COACH COULD LOVE,
FEBRUARY 3, 2019

ATLANTA—I'm a big fan of NFL Films.

Every year when the Super Bowl comes around, I enjoy watching the NFL Network, ESPN and whatever other channels show the 30-minute highlight films that chronicle the game's past champions.

While I can appreciate the historical significance of New England's 13-3 Super Bowl LIII win over the Los Angeles Rams on Sunday, it's going to be hard to watch these highlights again.

For much of the game, watching it was like having a root canal without Novocain.

In the world of high-scoring offenses, 400-yard passing games and wide receivers running wild, this was a slugfest that showed off two great defensive game plans that made field position paramount.

It was a game that produced the fewest points scored in Super Bowl history, and it's one only Patriot fans, and football coaches will likely appreciate—it featured defense, special teams and a timely running game.

Late in the third quarter, some of Cobb County's coaches chimed in with their opinion of the game. At the time, the game was tied 3-3, which also set a new record for fewest points scored through the first 45 minutes, and it looked like another field goal might be the difference.

McEachern coach Kyle Hockman broke the game down to its simplest terms.

"It was all about matchups," he said. "(It was New England coach) Bill Belichick against a young quarterback, and a great Rams defensive line against (Patriots quarterback Tom) Brady."

The New England defense dominated a team that averaged 33 points a game in the regular season and held them to a single field goal. Not once did the Rams drive inside the Patriots' 25-yard line, and they were held to 260 yards of total offense. To make matters worse, on three different occasions New England punter Ryan Allen had punts downed inside the Los Angeles 10.

The Rams defense was almost as good. It held the Patriots to only 13 points with a bend but don't break approach. If Los Angeles would have won, its MVP would have likely been punter John Hekker, who averaged 46.3 yards on nine punts, with a Super Bowl record 65-yard boot, with five punts downed inside the 20.

Late in the game, the Patriots channeled their best impression of the Kennesaw State Owls offense. Needing to run the ball to eat the final 4 minutes off the clock, Brady handed the ball to former Georgia running back Sony Michel seven of their last eight plays. The other play was a handoff to Rex Burkhead. New England drove from its 4-yard line, to the Los Angeles 24. The drive was 72-yards on nine plays. It and took 3:05 off the clock and led to the championship securing final field goal.

When I asked KSU coach Brian Bohannon, whose team was second in the country in rushing this past season, if it was nice to see a Super Bowl dominated by defense and special teams, he wasn't really sure. But when asked if it was nice to see an offensive line and running game slam the door on any potential comeback, it was an emphatic, "Yes!"

What was nice to see was Michel score the only touchdown of the game in his homecoming to Georgia. He finished the game with 18 carries for 94 yards.

As for the historical elements to the game, the Patriots won their sixth title, tying the Pittsburgh Steelers for most Super Bowls all-time.

Brady broke a tie with former San Francisco 49er and Dallas Cowboy Charles Haley, and now his sixth Super Bowl victory is more than any other player, and Belichick tied former Chicago Bears coach George Halas and the Green Bay Packers' Curly Lambeau for most championships as a coach.

There is little doubt Atlanta put on a great Super Bowl week. Falcons' president Rich McKay was quoted earlier Sunday that it likely won't take nearly two decades to get the Super Bowl back again.

However, Atlanta has to hope its next game features more action, big plays and scoring. Otherwise, Hillgrove coach Phil Ironside may have had the right idea all along. He didn't watch the game.

"I'm on a football fast," he said. (But 3-3 in the fourth quarter?) It sounds boring."

And it's why I will probably turn the channel when NFL Films debuts the highlights of Super Bowl LIII.

GHSA GETS IT RIGHT ... AND WRONG, MAY 14, 2017

Saturday afternoon at Lakewood Stadium in Atlanta, the Georgia High School Association appeared as if it was about to allow a state championship game to be contested on a playing field that was not properly set up with equipment that did not meet specifications.

Sound familiar?

Only this time, game officials alerted GHSA lacrosse administrator Denis Tallini that there were problems.

To Tallini's credit, he didn't say, "It's the same on both ends. Let's play ball," like the floor supervisor at last year's state basketball championship games did at the Macon Coliseum when notified the stanchions were set up a foot farther back than they should have been. Tallini tried to fix the problem.

Unfortunately, the Class A-AAAAA girls state championship lacrosse game was eventually postponed because the goals were not in championship condition and the field was not lined properly.

While Tallini faced the problem head-on, the situation the GHSA and the teams found themselves in should have never occurred, and there are a couple of questions that need to be asked.

First, why were the games scheduled at Lakewood Stadium in the first place? In the championship program, GHSA Executive Director Gary Phillips thanked Tallini for securing the location, but, according to Tallini himself, the stadium did not host a lacrosse game during the regular season.

Why not secure a venue for the biggest games of the year that consistently prepares for the sport that is being competed there? This was one of the many reasons the basketball tournament was moved from Macon to the University of Georgia and Georgia Tech this season. The Coliseum did not have any other basketball games scheduled for the venue.

But more than that, when it was asked if a GHSA representative was present when the field was prepared for play, Tallini's answer came across as mind boggling.

"I can't answer that," Tallini told the MDJ. "The Atlanta Public Schools were in charge of making the original setup. I don't know when they brought (the goals) in. Nonetheless, when we got here (Saturday), I didn't have an opportunity to inspect them, and I'm not an official, so I wouldn't know what was appropriate and what wasn't. The officials got here and said, 'We've got a problem with these goals,' and the coaches agreed to that.

"The original set of goals were brought in from another Atlanta school that plays lacrosse, and then we found that they were bent and that they were not appropriate, so we got another set. The second set was brought from Maynard Jackson, and those are the ones that we are working on now. We found out that they were using zip ties, and it wasn't properly laced, and that needed to be done, so that's what they're working on now."

"I didn't have an opportunity to inspect them."

How is it, for state championship events, the GHSA does not have someone on-site to make sure the field is set up and ready for action many hours, if not a day or two in advance, to make sure these kinds of blunders are avoided?

"I'm not an official, so I wouldn't know what was appropriate and what wasn't."

Also, especially after last year's basketball fiasco, how is it the GHSA has employees, let alone an administrator responsible for a sport, who does not know the proper setup for competition?

To the GHSA's credit, everything was fixed and the boys Class A-AAAAA championship game apparently went off without a hitch, and the Class 6A-7A games are scheduled for the same location on Saturday.

Unfortunately, that does little for the Kell and Blessed Trinity players, coaches and fans that expected to see their teams compete for a title only to see an entire day wasted because of incompetence.

Hopefully, wherever and whenever their game is played, it is set up properly, the weather is good, fans can get there and everything goes off perfectly, because they deserve it, and the GHSA should bend over backwards to make it happen.

CLASSIC CAR SEES NEW LEASE ON LIFE '56 DODGE TO BE DRIVEN AT DAYTONA, JANUARY 31, 2007

Bill Allen is bringing the '50s and the Pettys back to the beach at Daytona.

Allen has built a replica of Lee Petty's 1956 Dodge D-500-1, a car of which fewer than 100 ever existed, and will be taking it to Daytona next month. He will drive the car in the annual re-enactment of Daytona's Measured Mile in February and then have "The King," Richard Petty, and his brother, Maurice Petty, autograph the decklid.

Once the autographs are dry, it will complete a "labor of love," that Allen, a Kennesaw resident who has spent more than 40 years rebuilding more than 100 classic Porsches, has had in the works for over 10 years.

"In the mid-'90s I decided I would like to rebuild something American," said Allen, a 63-year old retired finance specialist from Lockheed-Martin. "Up till then, my entire life I had built customers cars and my kids cars. I had never built one for myself."

He knew he wanted to build something from the '50s, the time he was introduced to racing when his father would take him to Atlanta's Lakewood Speedway. It was the time when NASCAR was actually running true stock cars.

His selection of the Dodge came because of something he read on the back of a trading card before he began his project. It said: "Lee Petty and youngest son Maurice drove a 1956 Dodge to Phoenix, Ariz. Lee ran the car in a 150-lap race and finished fifth. The pair then drove the car home to Level Cross, N.C."

Allen had an opportunity to talk to the elder Petty about the project when he met Lee at a Living Legends of Auto Racing event. It was then his exuberance for the project took an early hit.

"I was excited about telling him about my idea of restoring and recreating his car," Allen said. "When I met him I said, 'I am restoring the

'56 Dodge Coronet D-500-1.' He told me, 'Nice car, I wish I had had one.'"

Allen knew Petty had driven one and had the pictures to prove it. He says he believes Petty did not understand what he was trying to tell him. Unfortunately, Petty died in April 2000 before Allen could begin the reconstruction process.

Allen turned his complete attention to the project in 2002, soon after his retirement. He started by getting approval from Richard Petty to create the car.

"Just do it," Allen said Petty told him.

With necessary approval, Allen started by buying a '56 Coronet D-500 sedan that he was going to turn into the replica. He then located an original engine in Fertile, Minn., a town 30 miles from the Canadian border. Once he arrived for the engine, Allen found something even better.

"The guy up there, Mopar Mel, said he had the body to go with the engine," Allen said. "It would not have appealed to me, but after matching the (serial) numbers with the Chrysler Museum, and I was able to confirm the construction date, I realized I couldn't stop."

The body had been in the junkyard since 1964, but Allen bought it and had the pieces painted and sent to him. Once the pieces arrived, he needed to fabricate new fenders, a hood, a decklid and floorboards, amongst other parts. He was able to salvage many of the original instruments, along with some of the chrome piping. During the next four-plus years, he slowly put the car together.

Allen was able to track down the original paint scheme in oriental coral and sapphire white. Then he sent the car to Ken Dillard in South Carolina, a master artist, to turn the sedan into Lee Petty's 1956 race car.

One of the final pieces installed was the new windshield. Unfortunately, Allen said the glass cracked during installation, so it will be imperfect for the trip to Daytona. But it's a setback Allen will have to live with.

"Many thousands of hours have gone into this car," he said. "And a significant amount of blood, sweat, tears and dollars."

Exactly how many dollars Allen refused to say.

Allen expects to travel to numerous car shows across the country showing off his completed trophy car during the next calendar year. Just how many will depend on Richard and Maurice Petty. Neither knows the car is complete or will be in Daytona next month. Allen expects both to be in attendance at the Legends dinner, but if not, he has a plan.

"It's become an obsession to get those autographs," Allen said. "If it fails I'll make a trip to Level Cross and stay in (Petty's) parking lot until I get it."

EFFORTS SIGNED, SEALED,
JULY 23, 2007

If nothing else, Bill Allen is persistent.

In January, we brought you the story of how Allen, a 63-year old Kennesaw resident who has restored classic Porsches for 40 years, had rebuilt a 1956 Dodge D-500 into a replica of Lee Petty's race car of that same year.

Allen's intention was to take the car to Daytona during the week of the 500, partake in the annual reenactment of the Measured Mile on fabled Daytona Beach, and put the finishing touches on the car by having Richard Petty and his brother Maurice Petty to sign the deck lid, i.e. the trunk lid. The signatures would validate Allen's effort and give him the keepsake of a lifetime.

There was one problem.

Although scheduled to attend that week's Legend's Dinner, where Allen was hoping to get Richard's signature, Petty was a no-show.

"It was the first time in four years he did not make the Legends' event," Allen said. "I was really bummed out."

However, there was no way Allen was not going to get his signatures. It just took him a little longer than he thought.

The '56 earned a reputation at the Measured Mile. Many people around North America wanted to see the vehicle, so Allen obliged over the last few months, taking it through the Midwest and into Canada, where literally, the third Canadian he met was a classic car lover—only it wasn't at a car show, it was at the border.

"When (the border agents) searched the trailer they came up and told me, 'We'll have to call our supervisor,'" Allen said. "I thought, 'Oh no, they are going to confiscate my car.'"

Instead, it was so the supervisor could admire the Dodge.

Allen took the car from Canada, back through the Great Lakes region to Tulsa, Oklahoma in June for another car show.

There he met a man by the name of "Snicker Dan" a man who raced against Lee Petty and his '56 Dodge in an event where legend had it that Petty—during the race—got out of his car and red flagged it, bringing it to a halt.

"Yep, it happened," Snicker Dan told Allen, who had a plaque that talked about that day which Allen had his new friend autograph. "I was in that race."

From Tulsa, Allen was to drive to Randleman, N.C., for another show—and another possible meeting with Petty. Only he almost missed his chance again because he lost the car's ignition key.

Not to be denied, Allen did what every self-respecting car man would do—in essence, he hot-wired it.

Petty was supposed to spend the day with the car enthusiasts in Randleman, but it was shortened to an hour because of another engagement in Charlotte. Allen would not have gotten King Richard's signature if not for a chance meeting in the parking lot outside the exhibition hall.

"I was about to take my car back to the trailer when I see Richard come out of the building," Allen said. "He started walking through some of the (show) cars and about that time he looked my way and said, 'I like that Dodge.'"

Finally, the signature verifying all Allen's hard work was his. There was only one possible thing could ruin it.

"Here I have this fresh signature and it starts to rain," he said. Then, he said his wife had her best idea when it came to one of his cars. "When I got it back to the trailer she said, 'Don't try wiping the deck lid off, let me get my hair dryer,' so we stood there while she blow dried the whole deck lid."

When the rain stopped, Allen decided to take the chance of taking the car up to Maurice Petty's engine shop in Level Cross, N.C. No one at the shop had seen Maurice for months, or knew how to get in touch with him, but Allen decided to try a last ditch effort. He opened the car in the parking lot putting it on display for anyone to see. It was then he saw an old, beat up, blue pickup truck coming across a farmer's field.

"Out of the blue, this old truck pulls up and it's Ritchie and Ramsey Petty, Maurice's son and grandson," Allen said. "I asked them do they think Maurice would like to see the car."

A few minutes later, Maurice, who suffers with polio, was there, looking at the car and confirming all the old stories, pictures and parts Allen had questions about. Better yet, Maurice signed the deck lid, on the opposite side from his brother.

It was about that time when another car came around the bend and the driver stopped and took interest in the gathering. It was Richard, back from his event in Charlotte.

For 45 minutes, the Petty brothers talked with Allen about the car. As far as their memories could recall, the only things on the Dodge that Allen missed were seat belt straps, and according to Richard, the tires.

"I'm not sure about those Firestones," Allen said Petty told him.

"We usually didn't have enough money to buy those. We usually ran on Montgomery Ward's."

Allen said with the quest for signatures complete, all he has to do is put on the clear coat to protect them. After that, he's taking the car—with a new ignition key—on tour so others can get the same kind of enjoyment looking at it, as he had building it.

Now when he talks to the admirers, he has more stories to tell.

MCCAIN'S SPORTS MUSINGS ARE WIDE-RANGING, JULY 6, 2014

ARLINGTON, Va.— Sen. John McCain is concerned with the direction big-time college football is heading. He said professionalism of the sport has taken over, and any appearance of competitive balance has been shattered.

"It's sad that you can pretty much tell which will be the top four teams before the season starts," McCain said.

It was just one of many topics he talked about while addressing the Associated Press Sports Editors' annual convention last week, just outside Washington.

"Is it really an amateur sport," he questioned, "when coaches are making (millions) of dollars a year?"

Most people know the 77-year-old five-term senator from Arizona and a two-time presidential candidate as a politician. Some may know him as a Navy pilot and war hero who was captured and tortured by the Viet Cong for nearly five years after being shot down.

But I doubt many know McCain as a passionate sports fan with a self-deprecating sense of humor.

"There was a Senator named Barry Goldwater from Arizona, and he ran for president," McCain said. "Then there was Rep. Morris Udall. He was from Arizona and ran for president. Former Gov. Bruce Babbitt, he was from Arizona and ran for president. And I am from Arizona, and I ran for president.

"Arizona may be the only state in the country where mothers don't tell their children they can grow up to be president of the United States."

McCain was a four-sport athlete at Episcopal High School in Alexandria, Va. He played football, baseball, tennis and wrestled. His sports career continued at the Naval Academy, where he made the wrestling team and took up boxing.

McCain was honest about his athletic prowess.

"Mediocre was the highest level I reached."

McCain also said he is concerned about performance-enhancing drugs, and how there's always someone in a laboratory trying to develop something that can't be detected by today's current testing. He also said he understands the draw potentially harmful substances are for today's athletes, who may need them to get to an elite level.

"When I was a midshipman at the Naval Academy, and someone would have told me I could play professional football just by taking a couple of these shots, the temptation would have been overwhelming, just like it is for many of the athletes today," he said.

McCain said he understood, with college football becoming big business, why the service academies can rarely compete on the national stage. But he couldn't help but to wax nostalgic as he thought back to 1963, when Roger Staubach and Navy played Texas in the national championship game.

McCain also touched on the current controversy in the nation's capital, about the Washington Redskins name. While he said he would not be in favor of any legislation forcing Redskins owner Daniel Snyder to change the team's name, he does wish Snyder and tribal leaders would sit down and have a real dialogue, and let common sense prevail.

"If the Native American community thinks it's offensive," McCain said of the Redskins name, "then it's offensive."

McCain wrapped up his 15-minute talk with a story that originated from an Esquire questionnaire he received at least 15 years ago. The final question of the survey asked who his greatest living hero was.

McCain's answer was Ted Williams. The questionnaire led to the senator having an opportunity to meet the greatest hitter who ever lived.

"We went down to his house in Orlando, and we had a long conversation," McCain said. "He kept wanting to ask me about politics, and I wanted to know about his relationship with Joe DiMaggio."

McCain said he eventually got around to talking about something they had in common. Both were combat fighter pilots.

Williams, who hit .344 with 521 home runs and 1,839 RBIs over a 19-year career with the Boston Red Sox, was commissioned as a second lieutenant in the U.S. Marine Corps as a Naval aviator and served the final three years of World War II as a flight instructor stateside. After the war, he joined the Marine reserves to help the unit with recruiting.

Williams later missed most of the 1952 and '53 seasons after he was brought back to active duty during the Korean War.

"John Glenn, the famous astronaut (and later senator from Ohio), was in the same squadron with Ted Williams in Korea and they flew missions together," McCain said. "And he said that Ted Williams was the best naval aviator that he knew. Now, that's quite a compliment coming from a man of John Glenn's caliber.

"On one of the missions, Ted Williams' plane got shot up. It's on fire and could not get its landing gear down and he did something really miraculous. He landed it in an outlying airfield, wheels up. He landed it safely and walked away.

"So, I asked him—I said, 'Why in the world didn't you just eject from the aircraft?'"

McCain likely knew the answer. On the day he ejected from his plane over Vietnam, McCain suffered two broken arms, a broken leg and then nearly drowned when he parachuted into a lake. He was then captured by the North Vietnamese and held captive for six years in a prisoner of war camp where he was tortured.

Williams' answer is likely why he was a hero to McCain, and to so many others.

"This guy looked at the canopy bows, the metal bars that the plastic lines up to," McCain said. "And remember, he was 6-foot-3, and he said, 'I looked at the canopy bows and knew, if I ejected, I would break both my knees, and I would never have played baseball again.'"

The story was a fitting end of one hero talking about another.

ORRVILLE OR COBB, HIGH SCHOOL SPORTS MARK HOME, JULY 21, 2014

ORRVILLE, Ohio—From downtown Cleveland the trip lasts about an hour and 15 minutes. You leave a major-metropolitan area and head south. As the miles go by one-by-one you begin to see gently rolling terrain and fields planted with corn, soybeans or maybe some freshly chopped hay.

As you near town it is hard to decide if this is the 1950s or 2013. The streets are lined with trees and World War II era houses. Kids ride their bikes in the neighborhood or spend the summer in the local park playing basketball or hanging out by the local pool. There is always a fast-pitch softball tournament going on and neighborhoods rotate having block parties. It's the kind of town which seems to remind people of a simpler time and place, right up to the point where one of those neighborhoods butt up against the local CVS, McDonalds or Taco Bell.

It's not quite Mayberry, but it's not metro-Atlanta either. It's Orrville, Ohio, population 8,395, and I call it home.

There are two major claims to fame from Orrville — the first, you see at the town limits on Highway 57 when you pass the big sign that says it is the proud home of former Indiana and U.S. Olympic basketball coach Bobby Knight.

The second, you learn about mere blocks later when you begin to pass the J.M. Smucker Company (and with a name like Smucker's, it has to be good), which takes up much of the downtown area.

And, it seems, after spending the week there, there were two prevalent topics of conversation — work, in which more than half the town is making your favorite jelly, jam, peanut butter (Jif), coffee (Folgers), shortening (Crisco) or any of the other multitude of products that line store shelves. (Go ahead, pick up the jar of grape jelly in your refrigerator. On the back of the label it says — J.M. Smucker Co., Orrville, Ohio, 44667. See, I told you so). The other topic is sports.

Orrville actually has a couple of ties to the Southeastern Conference. Current LSU football coach Les Miles grew up in Elyria, Ohio, and when he was in school, he would come in the summer and play in some of those fast-pitch softball tournaments at Orr Park. The other had a more direct reflection on the football field. Former Florida coach Ron Zook began his coaching career as a defensive backs coach for Orrville High School in 1976, but college football does not resonate in the area like it does in Cobb County.

Most people in this part of northern Ohio are Ohio State fans. They don't need to pay attention to things like SEC Media Days to get a feel for how each team in the conference may fare this season. They just want to know when the Buckeyes play Michigan.

And, while the return of LeBron James to the Cavaliers and the circus that is "Johnny Football" with the Browns is in full swing and holding people's interest, the most important thing Orrville sports fans want to know, like many of the fans in Cobb County, is how well their high school football team is going to play this upcoming season.

In fact, while I was walking around my old high school this week, it dawned on me that the sports programs in Orrville would fit in well in Cobb County. Football has always come first, but other sports on campus always seem to have more success. In Orrville's case, basketball has always been its calling card — and not just because of Coach Knight.

When I attended, the program always seemed to advance to the region championship game (the Sweet 16) but lose to a private school like Akron St. Vincent-St. Mary (the then-future high school of LeBron James).

Since then, Orrville has won three basketball state championships — 1992, '95 and '96. And, it is the only program in Ohio High School Athletic Association history to win back-to-back state titles, and have the second come in a higher classification.

When I was a junior in 1986, the football team advanced to the state championship game. It played in Ohio Stadium, also known as the Horseshoe, on the campus of Ohio State University — and lost.

It wasn't until 1998 when Orrville, quarterbacked by future Ohio State quarterback Justin Zwick, won a state championship in football.

Until 2011, it remained the only football state championship in Wayne County history.

However, this year, the fans in Orrville aren't expecting a state championship. Last year's squad is coming off a 1-9 season, arguably the worst showing in the program's 111-year history. And many of those fans are still complaining about the year-old Sprint Turf field the school installed — not because of the cost, but because heading into its second year of use, the team has yet to win on its new field.

But hope springs eternal. While I was there I heard about the players that would bring the team back to prominence.

Just like the players at Marietta, Allatoona, McEachern, Pope and all across Cobb County, those in Orrville were in the weight room, participating in 7-on-7s, and doing the necessary summer work that helps to make those lifelong memories in the fall.

It just proves, no matter where you go, high school sports form the ties that make wherever you live, a home.

DO YOU REALLY KNOW NOW
WHAT YOU THINK YOU WILL KNOW THEN?,
MAY 29, 2011

All the graduations are over.

The parties that go with them are a memory, too.

And for all you newly graduated seniors, for something you thought would never arrive, it was over pretty quickly. Wasn't it?

It doesn't seem all that long ago that you stepped inside your high school for the first time as a freshman. Everything was new, exciting and you hoped you would fit in with the upperclassmen. Two years went by quickly and, all of a sudden, you were the upperclassmen and playing the same jokes on the underclassmen that were played on you.

Now, it's going to start all over again.

While putting together the Scholar Athletes section, I was struck by a couple of things. For starters, if anyone thought you were going away to school by going to the University of Georgia, think again. Fifty-four of the 221 student athletes that filled out information sheets will be heading to Athens in the fall.

Maybe the dorms will have their own Cobb County wing.

And, for the second straight year, many of you want to become some kind of engineer.

I wish everyone luck.

Now the question is, will you finish where you start? And, will you actually be what you think you want to be?

In the end, neither answer will mean as much to you then as it does today.

I started my collegiate career at Tri-State University in Angola, Ind.

I went there on a golf scholarship and was going to leave four years later with a degree in economics.

The next semester I was majoring in marketing.

A year-and-a-half later I was at Cleveland State University.

Three months after that I was working in Birmingham, Ala.

Ten years later, I enrolled at UAB.

Why am I telling you this? Because it doesn't matter how you start—it's how you finish. Between point A and point B, you have the opportunity to learn a lot about yourself.

For all the engineering majors, you might get to school and find out it wasn't what you thought it would be. That's OK, as long as you find what it is that really interests you.

Once you get to college, you never know what or when that is going to happen.

I was on my fifth major before I realized I could be a sports writer. Even then I didn't graduate with a journalism degree. I got my degree in history.

For those 54 student-athletes who are going to Georgia, you might find out that it's not for you. That's OK, when I started college I never would have imagined I was going to land in Birmingham, but it ended up being home for 20 years. It's where I met lifelong friends, married my wife and found a career.

Now, I wouldn't suggest following my 17-year plan, and based on the information provided, the overwhelming majority of you won't have to worry. You are far more mature than I was at 18. But for those few who might be questioning yourselves, those who don't know where you are going to school yet, or what you want to be, don't worry, there's plenty of time.

The important thing is, when you do figure it out, do your best, follow through and finish.

Just like you did this week.

LOOKING BACK AT THE FAIRGROUND ERA,
AUGUST 3, 2018

When I first moved into my office at the Marietta Daily Journal there was a book in my desk.

It was the Encyclopedia of Sports. The book spelled out everything you ever needed to know about sports from the turn of the 20th century to 1950. On the inside cover, it was signed, "Property of Horace Crowe, Sports Editor, Marietta Daily Journal 1955."

That book made the trip from the MDJ offices on the Marietta Square to the brand new, state-of-the-art offices on Fairground Street. The year was 1970.

For those of you who remember the '70s, things had a tendency to be gaudy. I never got to see it in person, but the paper may have had the definition of gaudy with its giant Marietta Daily Journal sign that anyone coming down Fairground Street, South Cobb Drive or Atlanta Road could see. It was so big it rivaled the "Big Chicken" as a Marietta landmark.

The sign was indicative of the new publisher. Otis Brumby, Jr. had assumed the role of publisher in 1967, and over time, he grew, like the paper, to be one of the largest and most respected pillars of the Cobb County community.

In my dealings with Mr. Brumby, he was a no-nonsense presence who demanded excellence and transparency. Because of that, and his dogged news sense, the MDJ became the must read for politicians, business owners, those interested in what was going on in their community, and sports fans of our local high schools and universities.

Mr. Brumby surrounded himself with other local legends of the industry.

From before the time Mr. Brumby became publisher, until after his death in 2012, Bill Kinney was the eyes, ears and soul of the paper. He forgot more about Cobb County history than historians could write about.

Kinney covered everything, knew everybody and broke more news than Twitter. He was able to pass that knowledge on to Joe Kirby, who took Kinney's baton and ran with it. Unfortunately, he was taken from us much too soon.

The three men made up the editorial board of the MDJ for nearly two decades. They tackled the tough issues. There weren't many days that didn't have at least one or more of them grilling local politicians from the local school boards and city councils to gubernatorial candidates, senators and on occasion, presidential candidates. For some, an invite to the conference room at the Fairground St. office was viewed as "their turn in the barrel."

Times change, and so do needs.

Our readership is evolving from the hands on ink and newsprint that has been delivered to their driveways every day to news consumers with computers, smart phones and tablets.

No longer does the building on Fairground Street rumble each night when the press fires up. In fact, there isn't a printing press on site anymore as the printing of all Times-Journal Inc. newspapers was consolidated at the Rome News-Tribune.

The building that used to house hundreds of people that provided our readers with the daily news is much too large for our current staff. The MDJ is streamlining.

As of last Thursday, we are no longer on Fairground Street. We are moving back to Marietta Square, where everything started in 1866.

In fact, it's like fulfilling a final wish for Mr. Brumby, who I've heard would never have left the Square if it would have been his initial decision.

We once again are moving into a state-of-the-art location. The new MDJ offices are at 47 Waddell Street. Everything is new, crisp and clean with the latest in digital technology.

Our new building is the former Cobb County Board of Elections building, which seems like a perfect fit, considering election nights are those that make our newsroom sing.

But just because we have new digs, it doesn't mean our focus on quality community journalism is going to change.

I'm sure when the reporters moved into the new building on Fairground St., they wondered if they would have the opportunity to cover big stories like the Atherton Drug Store explosion on the Square in 1963.

Well, thanks to Mr. Brumby, Kinney, Kirby and the other talented journalists that worked there over five decades, the answer was yes. There was the Cobb County School District laptop scandal that cost superintendent Joe Redden his job in 2005, the massive flooding that cost so many families their homes in southern parts of the county in 2009, and even a sports story that told how the Georgia High School Association couldn't set up the baskets properly and screwed up the state championship basketball games in 2016.

Of course, arguably the biggest story in the history of the paper, and the county, happened on Nov. 11, 2013. It was a day that the building on Fairground shook, the phones rang off the hook, and the MDJ was the national publication of record and the first to report the Braves' move to Cobb County.

It was the kind of day that made us proud to be journalists. It was the kind of day that Mr. Brumby would have loved to see, just like his father before him.

Otis Brumby III is our publisher now. He has said this move is like getting back to our roots. We are a community paper returning to the heart of the community—the Marietta Square.

But just like the way Mr. Brumby, Kinney, Kirby and the journalists that came before us deserve our thanks, so does the building on Fairground.

They did good work there, and like their memories, the old building will not be forgotten anytime soon.

We did good work there, and we bring their legacy, along with the Encyclopedia of Sports, with us to Waddell Street. It's time to record more history and write our names in the books that will be there for the next generation.

We're coming home to the Square, and it's time to get to work.

John Bednarowski is the sports editor of the Marietta Daily Journal and former president of the Associated Press Sports Editors. He has been honored with more than 70 state and national writing awards. He has been recognized as the best columnist in Georgia a combined 10 times by the Georgia Sports Writers Association and the Georgia Press Association, and he was recognized as the best columnist in the country at small newspapers by the Associated Press Sports Editors in 2019.